SEven YEARS in an ORANgE HoVeRCRAft

A victory from **adolescence** to **maturity**

CANDACE ANNE

WESTBOW
PRESS®
A DIVISION OF THOMAS NELSON
& ZONDERVAN

WestBow Press books may be ordered through booksellers or by contacting:

WestBow Press
A Division of Thomas Nelson & Zondervan
1663 Liberty Drive
Bloomington, IN 47403
www.westbowpress.com
844-714-3454

ISBN: 978-1-6642-2361-5 (sc)
ISBN: 978-1-6642-2363-9 (hc)
ISBN: 978-1-6642-2362-2 (e)

Library of Congress Control Number: 2021902878

Print information available on the last page.

WestBow Press rev. date: 04/16/2021

CONTENTS

Acknowledgements 1
Why Me, Why Now, Why Ever, Why the Title? 7

Part One **51**

First area pride affected: career 51
Second area pride affected: relationships ....,,. 80
Third area pride affected: identity – before 103

Part Two **107**

The big reveal – what's really under the cover 107

Part Three **153**

At first the truth hurts … and then it shall set you free 153
New identity: after & going forward 215

Bibliography 233

ACKNOWLEDGEMENTS

This book was written for the Glory of God.

-

"I will praise You, O LORD, with my whole heart;
I will tell of all Your marvelous works.
I will be glad and rejoice in You;
I will sing praise to Your name, O Most High."
Psalm 9:1-2 NKJV

-

And for my loving and dedicated parents who deserve an apology and explanation for what I put them through, during my *decade of despair and wandering.*

To my Dad, I miss you. I have always loved spending time with you because you are so pleasant and peaceable to be with, which is why I cherish our chatty phone conversations so much. Thank you for imparting on me a great deal of who you are, I really love this side of me. From a young age I watched you sitting in a quiet spot, reading page after page, highlighting the words of a book and then reflecting on them. All with the intention to apply what you had learnt. This simple act has impacted me in wondrous ways, as I developed the same awareness to reflect and seek personal growth through reading. You have trained your children well in this and have inspired each of us to think with insight and respond to situations with maturity and wisdom. I also cherish how well you have always provided for your family so well, granting us a stable and secure homelife – a gem in the pursuit of peace I have come to realise. I also value how active you've always been by continually working on many projects with your own hands. Whether it is building a wall, a house, or a wooden bench, your natural ability and years of experience shine through demonstrating how much can be achieved with hard work and applying oneself diligently. You have taught me so much about the fruit of labour. Thank you for your loving patience and thoughtful quiet guidance whenever I needed it. You have a been a model father to your children Dad, and I love you. May our Lord be with you.

Mom, words cannot describe the thanks I have for you. You planted a seed in me, nurtured it and helped it grow. You have no idea how much impact you have had on me as Candy. I am so very grateful for every ounce of hard work and time you invested into me, your own marriage, my childhood and our family. Your daily walk with the Lord and courageous hardworking attitude towards life has taught me to endure and persevere through all of my tough times. It is your can-do attitude and zest for life that helps give me confidence. Mom's and daughters really do have a special bond, I think it's because we're so similar in so many ways. Before having children of my own I never fully grasped the depth of a mother's love, as well as the charge one develops for building a fulfilling life. Not only for yourself but also for your whole family. I could write pages and pages on the fantastic environment you and Dad generated for the basis for an unforgettable childhood, something I recollect daily to implement myself. As I reflect on you as my mom, not one of your efforts, prayers and inputs has gone unnoticed. Your hardworking hands-on approach, courage and resourcefulness have been indelible in shaping my character. I can't wait for this next chapter to begin. Only God knows what's in store. I love you. May our Lord be with you.

Mom and Dad. You should write a book on marriage because your version of it is so admirable. I love that you are best friends, and that you challenge each other to grow in all areas, especially in the Lord's wisdom. At the same time, you allow each other the space to thrive as individuals. Thank you for showing me what is worth fighting for and preparing me for the enduring duty and pleasure of marriage so well. I thank the Lord for you as role models. I love you.

To my brother and sister. Still today we share such a close bond because of the tight family unit we grew up in as children. Mom and Dad have cultivated these connections so maturely and devotedly. I am so proud of you both as you are both outstanding individuals whose love for God is so clear and so fruitful. What a privilege it is to know you both, and to call you my special bro and sis. Each of you, in your unique and special way, has helped me grow in my faith in ways that have shaped me tremendously, thank you for this. You have each taught me so much about myself, helping me to iron out my rough edges. I love you. May our Lord be with you.

My beloved husband. What do I say to my knight in shining armour, who continues to be my wonderful provider and protector? Venturing through our simple lives together with you has been eventful to say the least. We have endured courageously with God's strength and with perseverance, so will make it to the end together. I am so grateful for you. You have been a gift from Heaven above. Your strength of character, wisdom, firm integrity and generous serving heart are traits I fell in love with and continue to cherish. Thank you for your hours and hours of sacrifice, as well as your blessing as I put this book together. I couldn't have done this without you, in more ways than one. Here's to the next chapter my love. I love you. My prayer is that this story touches and enriches the lives of others so they too may see how Great our God is. May our Lord be with you and shine His face upon you.

To my extraordinary children. You are so alive! So vibrant, so present, so happy, always up for a laugh and a game. I love watching you adventure through your little worlds. Especially in those moments when you care for the needs of one another and others beyond your own. This shows me how much of who you are and how I want your heart to be: giving, selfless, caring and kind. The Lord blessed me richly when each of you were born because you have taught me so much about the most exciting thing in my life: learning about who created us. Mommy adores you two, and may you see this book as a testimony to how much I have loved walking with our Lord and Saviour. My prayer is that you two find the same unending fulfilment that flows from His living waters. I love you. May our Lord be with you and keep you daily from harm.

My genuine thanks to the rest of my extended family: my very special Gran, aunts, uncles, and cousins who have unknowingly shaped me in one form or another. Your support and love while still a child, then into adolescence, and now adulthood is treasured. Thanks also to my in-laws, both *adopted* sisters, and beautiful nieces. It is good to be a part of you all.

To my sisters in Christ who have each come along my path at God's timing to impact me as needed. I have been blessed endlessly by each one of you. Thank you.

***

I would also like to thank the team at Westbow Press for their patience and assistance in helping me realise my dream of sharing this story. What a great experience it has been working with you.

As well as Annemarie, a special friend and wonderful go-to graphic designer. I really appreciate all your help and support with this endeavour.

Thank you, and may you be blessed x

When sharing about yourself,
you must be willing to share all of it:
the good, the bad, and the ugly.
Pride will help no one.

WHY ME, WHY NOW, WHY EVER, WHY THE TITLE?

WHY ME?

I have written this book because I always knew that I would. If that makes any sense. Throughout the middle of the suffocating anguish, in the place where I couldn't even see my own hand because of the darkness. Something kept nudging at me, kept prodding at me, that one day I would write about what I was going through.

Something kept stirring that all of the hardship I was enduring. All of the agony I was pushing through, all the heartache, all the frustration, the confusion, the isolation, and dark loneliness was not in vain. I felt that one day the purpose of my trial would be revealed. Through it all, I never felt that any of the confusion and painful desperation was pointless. Somehow, I knew there was a purpose to all of my suffering. A greater purpose lay before it seemed.

There is a reason why all of this is happening to me. I would continually reassure myself. *There has to be a reason, there just has to be. I can't possibly be this lost or confused by chance without there being a bigger reason for it all. There must be someone or something or some force restricting me from moving forward in the various directions I am choosing because every path I take is being blocked off and rerouted. Nothing seems to be working. I feel like I'm being pushed and pulled from side to side and every route I attempt I am confronted with a brick wall already built to stop me. Why is this happening? It doesn't seem like it's happening to anyone else. Why am I feeling so inadequate all the time, like a failure? Why does everyone else seem to 'get it', and I don't? Why do I feel so stupid and useless, so empty and full of resentment? Who can I blame for these feelings? Why am I on the verge of breaking? What is keeping me together? Why does everyone else seem to know what's going on and I don't? Why do all their lives seem so stress-free and well-balanced and mine isn't? It's as if they signed up to receive the manual for success and I didn't even have a postal address. Why did my peers, friends and colleagues turn right at the fork in the road and I turned left? Why did they all seem to 'get' what I couldn't? It all seems to come so easily to everybody else.*

This concept of standing at a crossroads with me choosing the wrong road to take actually formed part of the original title of this book, "You take a left and I'll take a right". This phrase expressed how I felt because I continuously noticed how everybody else seemed to know how to do everything so well and I didn't. They seemed to whiz right passed me on the smooth side of the road while I crawled over the speed bumps and potholes on my side. Everyone else knew which way to turn, but I didn't. *Why do my choices not work out? I am hopeless. I am so lost.*

WHY NOW?

The book itself, its message rather, is ready to be written.

In an earlier version of this book, I tackled the material with the incorrect intention and from the wrong point of view. Needless to say, it fell to pieces like a flimsy craft project. In that first version it became tiring to write anything. This left me feeling unmotivated and even more hopeless than I already was. There seemed to be always something more appealing or pressing to do, and the act of writing never felt fluid. As a writer, this fluidity is vital because it is in this moment that you recognise you are writing something worthwhile, but with that version the words never came. The sentences never flowed automatically, and the content and material were jagged and non-sensical. It had bits and pieces of dotted memory struggling to form a paragraph. Nevertheless, this sad-little attempt at a book ended itself and one more time after that, so here I am, third time round. *Finally!*

In order for this version to reach almost 200 pages, something catalytic happened that would turn my third attempt into the final one. You'll have to keep reading to find out what it was, and how powerful this catalyst was.

When I glimpse at the first two attempts, I can't help but blush because they are simply too embarrassing to read, even for me. Both were a collection of silly and immature thoughts that dangled randomly on a page, proving just how juvenile my thinking was and where my intentions lay. I was lacking in fullness and the truth was missing: the real truth.

Eventually, when I finally undertook to write the book years after my two self-focussed attempts, the words simply slid from my fingertips … and here we are, third time round.

WHY EVER?

I must share what has happened and what continues to happen in order to benefit, strengthen and inspire others.

WHY THE TITLE?

The Chevy, the scooter, the driving, the cry!

Wandering is defined as walking slowly around or to a place, often without any particular sense of purpose or direction.

THE CHEVY

In 2006, I bought my first car. It was a brand-new orange Chevy Spark. It was in this vehicle where I retreated to when the pressure of my confusion became too much. For me the car was like a bubble of escape from the outside world, which was quite an appropriate description. It could have floated given the chance considering it was so lightweight. Slight gusts of wind often jolted the car quite forcefully whilst driving and whenever I noticed a windy swirl of spiralling leaves in the road up ahead, I would slow down because I knew what was coming: a sudden unsettling slight lift. The vehicle barely weighed eight hundred kilograms and when combined with a speed of say one hundred twenty kilometres per hour, it would shake and take off partly. Scarily, it felt as if it was hovering above the tarmac. My father and brother even lifted the entire car once instead of re-parking it - that's how light the tinny bodywork was.

Whenever I felt confused, directionless, miserable, or angry, I would climb into my orange bubble … and drive. I drove everywhere, and I mean everywhere and at any time. The South African province of Gauteng was my twenty-four hour drive through. I covered almost the whole area of this eighteen thousand square kilometre province. The M1 highway to Sandton, the M1 highway to Rosebank, the R24 to Johannesburg, the N1 back to Pretoria, the R21 past the airport, the R21 to East Rand Mall, the N1 back to Sandton, the N1 back to Centurion, the R585 past Olifantsfontein, the N1 to Rivonia, the Linksfield turnoff to Edenvale, the Kempton Park turnoff to Edenvale, Elgin Road under the bridge, Commissioner Street in Kempton Park, the R25 past Greenstone Mall in Edenvale, the R25 from Edenvale to Kempton Park. One hundred thousand kilometres later, and I still wasn't going anywhere.

Nine times out of ten, I didn't even have an appointment to attend or a reason to drive any of these routes, I simply drove in search of answers. Most often, there was no valid reason for me to spend forty minutes to two hours in traffic on any one of these journeys, but I did it willingly. The ridiculous part is I would actually spend only twenty minutes in the town or city I had driven to, even if it had just taken me forty minutes to get there, buy a pack of cigarettes and drive back to where I had come from, smoking all the way back while blasting my music. The driving had become a refuge for me. A means to feeling some form of productivity, and purpose for the day. I had somewhere to go when I turned on the ignition, somewhere to be, even if I really didn't. I guess it was therapeutic. The driving did serve a purpose. Even if it was really senseless. *How bewildered I was.*

These seven years spent driving in the Chevy I consider to be my *salad days.* These are the days referred to by Shakespeare as the youthful ones, accompanied by inexperience, enthusiasm, idealism, innocence, and carelessness. In my case these were all too true.

My inexperience was outside of what I was accustomed to. So, anything other than what I had been exposed to in the home and while growing up was completely foreign to me and so caught me off guard. Anything different and new in this outside world naturally seemed exciting, and I was curious to discover what all the fuss was about. The Chevy was my ticket to finding it. My golden ticket 'out of here", *I recall using these words.* My ticket out of here to discover where I fitted in and where the answers laid. The Chevy initiated the solution for my desperate itch for self-discovery. It was a vessel within which I could pop my head out from under the warm shelter of safety and poke around at the uncharted surroundings.

This act of driving became an essential part of my emancipation because I was then able to make my own choices about my day. I was especially able to make choices regarding my own movement. So instead of being reliant on others for transport, which always left me feeling stranded and cut off as if a part of me was *amputated,* I was now able to move freely. I wanted the freedom to choose whether I would attend a function or not and when I would leave or arrive. I also craved the responsibility surrounding such decisions because when one feels responsible for even the smallest details of your life, you become more accountable in other areas too.

To me, there was nothing more disheartening than waiting around for lifts and being stuck without a means of mobility. In a way, being unable to mobilise myself blocked the corridor to where I wanted to be at that stage of my life. This mobility was a big deal for me. I needed it. Being responsible for my own transport was vital to my zest for 'getting ahead' and 'finding where I needed to be', I would say. Not moving forward left me feeling unproductive and stagnant. Even though these longings would seem insignificant to someone who has had freedom of movement and independence for most of their life, it's a big deal to someone searching for a chance to see more and find out what the answers were. *Where did the answers lie?*

Once I had finally purchased the Chevy, I really disliked, even detested, having to ride with anyone else because that *feeling of amputation* bubbled up every time I climbed into the back seat of another person's car. Especially when I knew I could have driven there myself. I am not sure why this driving was so important to me. And so, it happened that I would even drive out of my way to pick my friends up for a night out, just so that I was the one driving, and not the one being driven. Being *amputated*, then sacrificing, then saving up money, then finally owning my own vehicle, and then not being free to move, chopped me up almost instantly. It was a no go, and I couldn't have it!

The sacrificing part came where I saved up for many months of salary to buy a car. Eventually after ten months of saving I still didn't own one and still wasn't independent enough. So, I used my car savings to buy a scooter which would in the interim allow me to get from A to B. Seven months later, I sold the scooter and used the money from the sale as a deposit for the car. One word to describe the scooter experience - juvenile!

THE SCOOTER

I remember *scootering* to gym one day with both my cousin and I on the scooter. However, I did not own two helmets, so we shared the helmet and took turns in wearing it. *If this is not juvenile then I'm not sure what is.* On the way back from the gym that was three point six kilometres from my house, the scooter gave one last, lousy puff and packed up. We ended up pushing the bike the whole way back home while poking fun at my choice in choosing a brand of scooter that neither of us had ever heard of. Cheap and unpopular, not the best combination. *On the bright side, we got a double work out that day.*

Yes, a bad choice in hindsight, but when you are young you aren't really worried too much about the future because you have so much of it ahead of you. And you have plenty of time to correct your mistakes. I should have seen the red flag of bad choices flapping wildly on the day I arrived at the bike shop to make my purchase. But because I was stubbornly blinded by my search for independence, I didn't even think twice about the possible risks. A sensible person would have turned around when greeted at reception by an ink-stained skinhead dotted in piercings who then offered to show them his backyard workshop where he assembled the bikes. Not me, I went right for it. Denying every intuitive urge to leave. *I was so eager to jump on this train of independence and search for answers that I pushed forward regardless of all the flashing warning signals that were appearing right before me.*

After this brief encounter at reception, I followed this man (who I had just met) all alone like a puppet to the back of the large property on which the shop was situated. On the walk we happened to snake through the graveyard of the biking world. On either side of us, stacked as high as the scarcely visible neighbouring rooftops were assorted piles of severely damaged motorbike and scooter parts. From burnt up chasses to mangled exhaust pipes, from worn out tyres to skew handle bars. Before me stood a backdrop to a side of life I had no experience with and was about to enter for the sake of searching for answers. At this point one would think I would've turned around and hotfooted it out of there after seeing this gloomy introduction to a life that lay before me ... but I didn't.

After arriving at his isolated workshop at the back of the property and with no one else in sight or earshot, the bike mechanic, donned in sleeveless leathers, began demonstrating how he assembled every bike that the shop sold. Not a clever sales pitch considering we had just meandered through the ultimate valley of machine death, but he continued talking anyway. After explaining how each bike arrived in bits and pieces from the Far East, he then invited me to go riding with him and the rest of the bike gang the following weekend. Picturing myself at a bike rally had the element of intrigue but then he proceeded to inform me that four riders were killed at the previous month's ride down to the city of Nelspruit. Tempting as it sounded (sarcasm intended), I thankfully still had several scruples of sense drifting around in my brain even after embarking on this sabotaging search for independence, and declined the offer. After handing over the hard-earned cash for the scooter at reception, I left the bike shop located in the dodgiest street of Kempton Park and headed home. Not only was the area notorious for its shady underworld, it was known for *shystering* twenty-something year old girls into buying knock-off scooters.

The scooter is a dicey form of transport and until you have ever ridden one, you are ignorant to the pitfalls of riding solo. Firstly, the rider is completely exposed to every kind of natural force. When it rains, you are rained on. When it's scorching hot outside, you suffer while the guy in the Volvo next to you blasts the cool air conditioner in comfort. There was many a time when the clouds above suddenly burst open and I'd have to endure the cold beating rain or find the nearest filling station under which to take shelter. Either way one's journey is interrupted. Secondly, the distance between you and the tarmac below is not far at all. If you fall, that rough road surface would surely sandpaper your skin severely. I won't even begin to explain the probability of survival if hit by a car driving at a high speed. So, when a close friend of mine, an avid biker himself, took a look at my helmet, the stunned look on his face said it all.

"How much did you pay for this helmet?" he asked me.

"About R150 (Aus$15)," I said.

"Just look here," and as he spoke, he peeled the inner lining from the colourful plastic outer covering and revealed a thin white layer of polystyrene foam.

"This!" pointing to the flimsy half-cardboard material in shock, "is what is protecting your head."

His words hit me like icy water when I realised how I had been played for a fool. How could that mechanic at the bike shop feel okay with selling me a helmet that never would have protected my head in the event of an accident? The inside was merely polystyrene. I hadn't known any better, but he had. If I had been killed, he would have been none the wiser and my parents would have been the ones to suffer, not him. And here I was making hasty self-centred decisions without their approval and blessing which could in reality have led to serious heartache and struggle for my loved ones.

Thinking back some twelve years to that sobering display of hard reality that my friend imparted that day, divulges how pathetically oblivious I had become to the consequences of my actions. I was so obsessed with my own desires that I had swept everyone else's feelings and concerns completely aside. In basic terms, my desperate search for answers was more serious than I thought. People in general make bad decisions when they're desperate, and will often resort to almost any measure to deliver them from their state of helplessness. But to put your life in harm's way like I did, was plain stupidity.

It didn't take long after that to come up with more than half the deposit for the car. So, when I finally saw that last bit of money come in, I drew it all. With ten thousand rand in hard cash, I drove straight to the car dealership and handed over my savings. The consultant still asked me why I didn't transfer the money electronically instead of carrying it on me. *Good question considering the route to the dealer was through an unsafe centre of town.* Another example of how I was once again just too blindly enthusiastic at this prospect of independence. *Again, with the stupidity! At least there would be no more sketchy scooter and ridiculous helmet.*

THE DRIVING

One of the reasons why I drove so much in my twenties was because the act of moving forward seemed purposeful. I had a goal when I drove. There was purpose and a predictable momentum to getting into my car. Switching on the ignition, putting on my sunglasses, locating my lighter, opening the box of Peter Stuyvesant blues, drawing the chosen smoke from the box, lighting the cigarette, inhaling that first drag, putting in petrol, changing lanes, hooting at bad drivers, listening to the radio, singing along to the lyrics, arguing with the radio show hosts, thinking aloud, talking to myself, passing landmarks, reaching destinations and then driving back again. On some days I'd even choose a different route, just to spice the entire day up. I'd then return later on in the day to wherever I was living at the time, with a growing hollowness.

(I have since quit smoking completely as my thirsting emptiness was replaced by something far greater. Smoking is also unhealthy and addictive.)

This phase of sporadic and erratic movement during my twenties didn't stop with my sporadic driving rituals but crept its way into how often I moved residences as well. This was yet another issue where I went left and everybody else went right - I just couldn't get settled. At one point I was in between living somewhere and who knows where so I drove around for a long while with most of my clothes in the car, including my grocery items. On one occasion when visiting a friend who needed sauce with the pasta she had cooked for us, I simply unlocked my boot and took out the sweet chilly dip. *Living from their car, who does that?*

You sometimes wish you could disappear, but
all you really want is to be found.

At some point I had just started renting a backyard flat and had been there for just over a month when the owners of the property began packing up to move out. They were out sooner than expected, leaving me alone on a dark empty property all by myself. *Another stupid decision: to continue renting a place that has been sold and still choosing to stay there all alone.* Night time was the worst because the main house lights were obviously off causing most of the property to fall in an eery darkness. The flat was so spacious that even the windows were more like doorways - a perfect entry way for thieves. So, between me and the two rescued kittens I had brought with from the previous place, and after putting up the good fight of bravery for about twenty minutes huddling on the couch. I couldn't stand the stress any longer and decided to exit the building. We retreated to the safest place I knew - my car. That night was the first night I spent in the good ol' Chevy. Somehow, I felt safer in the delicate Chevy then I did inside the flat with its brick walls and lockable doors. I deliberately slept in the driver's seat so that I could start the engine quickly and get the car moving in the dreaded event of a burglar breaking into the car during the middle of the night, which was a huge probability in South Africa. Even with the car's flimsy exterior, fragile framework and it's almost non-existent security measures, my orange bubble of safety was more appealing than a building full of access points. At this point you might be thinking, why didn't she just call somebody and stay with them for the night. The answer is simple - pride. I was too proud to admit that I had made yet another bad choice and more so that I was not coping. *Wow, the delusion of fighting for independence!*

Even though I wandered across Gauteng for many months, in search for answers and individuality, the one ingredient of the *salad days* I found came easily was the ingredient of enthusiasm and optimism. I remained optimistic, even on the hardest days. Thank goodness I had an expectant spirit because if not I would have suffered a great deal more as a result of the despondency. This optimism was grounded in the hope I had for my future and that it would eventually arrive. I just didn't know how to get there or where I would find it. Perhaps one of the reasons why I drove so much was because I thought I would arrive at my future even by chance or see the exit on a road sign next to the motorway. I thought the more I drove the more I would be in a position to stumble upon the place I was meant to be, with perhaps my future laying around the next corner. The problem with this – there were so many corners.

I remember one day in particular where I drove through an upmarket residential area of Brooklyn in Pretoria gazing at each house as I drove passed. I considered every house and imagined the possible future that could come from each one. Maybe, just maybe the person who lived in one of those houses would walk outside into their driveway and call out to me because my future was waiting inside.

On those days I simply rode up and down the streets in bafflement, wandering why and how I had missed the mark so completely. Everyone else seemed so busy, so productive, so purposeful and so co-ordinated. I also wanted to feel like that. I remember an occasion where I bought a large pizza and drove to the local sports fields. There I sat in the car chomping away at my double cheese with extra toppings hoping to see a sports practise take place. I thought that by watching people train, I would get a hint of the right direction to take in my life. As if their goal-orientated sportiness would inspire me as to what my purpose was. *I was so lost. How could I be this lost?*

The years spent wandering through the urban desert of despair during my early twenties - searching beyond its skyline for a sign - I really could have been carjacked or involved in a major accident, kidnapped or even worse in the car of mine because I was absurdly and shamefully reckless. I would drive over the speed limit and find it amusing because I didn't think the car could even move that fast. I would drive by myself at three o'clock in the morning after leaving a party and sometimes with the fuel tank almost on empty. Often, I would drive around in the middle of the night and in dark secluded unfamiliar areas. My car could have broken down during any one of these lonely travels and I most likely wouldn't have had airtime on my phone or a full battery to make any kind of call. Reflecting on how reckless I was during these years, I just shudder. So many wicked people could have come my way during these irresponsible night time quests, but somehow, they didn't. *Thank the Lord.*

Many a night my mom struggled to reach me via phone, either because I ignored her calls or because I was out somewhere and didn't hear the phone. I also carelessly forgot to return her calls and messages to console her. I justified this behaviour by saying that I was trying to *establish boundaries between my parents and my new independent self. How juvenile!* During the early hours of one morning, she contacted my landlord because she couldn't reach me but when he didn't see my car in the driveway she panicked and started calling my friends who also didn't know where I was. Needless to say, the next day I had an inbox full of messages from friends asking if I was okay and whether

I'd spoken to my mother. *How embarrassing!* They weren't supposed to know either. They weren't supposed to know how ridiculously confused I was. No one was supposed to know of my erratic behaviour. I tried to hide it but sometimes I slipped up. I am so sorry I put my dear parents through that ordeal. They didn't deserve any of it.

There I stood detached from anything that made sense. I craved a remedy to all of this. Anything that had the faintest whisper of an answer. I was desperate and lost. I hated it.

While staying in a commune at the age of twenty-two, I climbed into my car at midnight one evening to drive to the nearest internet café simply to check my Facebook account (because smart phones weren't out yet and Facebook was still new). The dangerously stupid part was: I didn't inform a single housemate that I was going anywhere. The stupidity gets even worse because in order to get to the café I had to park in a lonely semi-lit street followed by a secluded walk through a dark passageway. Not many decent people roam the streets that late at night so if I had been attacked, or even killed, nobody would have known until the morning. South Africa has among the highest violent crime rates in the world, anything could have happened to me. *Unless you are self-centred, confused, lost, or erratic, who does this kind of thing?*

It felt like I was chewing on a fresh lemon. If I didn't find a way to climb out of this hole I would die of dark bitterness.

It was in this Chevy that I was allowed to wander safely across Gauteng in search for answers to the many questions I had burnin' in my soul. *Why didn't I have a clue as to where I was supposed to live? Why didn't I know which career path to follow? Why didn't this decision come easily to me? Why was I struggling to finish my undergraduate degree? Why was everyone else progressing in their studies and I wasn't? Why was I procrastinating so much? Why was I battling to pass my LLB Law modules? Why wasn't I phased about my assignments or studying for exams? Why didn't I know what my purpose was? Why did I feel torn working in the places that I did? Why was I battling to enter the right kind of relationship? Why was I lying about my relationships? Why couldn't I find a boyfriend that my parents approved of? Why did I feel like an outsider at university? Why couldn't I land a cushy job like some of my friends had? Why did everyone else seem to know where they were going in life and I didn't? Why did I have a negative body image? Why was one mistake leading to many other bad choices? Why was I dying inside? Why was I lying to everyone else about this? Why was I lying to myself? Why couldn't I get a break? Why did nothing make sense? Why was everything so hard? Why was I smoking so much? Why did I feel so hopeless? Why was I feeling so lonely and so alone? Why did I hate living my life? Why did I fabricate my reality and present a false one to others? Why was I feeling so lost?*

THE CRY

And finally. After I had nothing else left in me. It was in my car, in my orange Chevy where I first cried out to God - and He answered.

In my distress I called to the Lord;
I cried to my God for help.
From his temple he heard my voice; my cry
came before him, into his ears.
- Psalm 18:6

NOBODY BUT ME

Nobody but me could see the tears staining my cheeks.

Nobody but me and the blaring radio could hear me shouting in a broken voice.

Nobody but me could see me slamming my fists on the steering wheel while struggling to breathe.

Nobody but me knew how much I was hiding, how much I was covering up.

Nobody but me knew of my hopelessness and the silent suffering I was battling with. I wasn't coping and nobody could help because nobody knew.

Nobody ever saw my fear, they couldn't have, I wouldn't let them see it.

I was throbbing with guilt from the lies I was covering up. I was lost and writhing in distress.

How many roads did I have to travel down to reach an answer? How many corners did I have to turn before I knew which road was the right one? How much distance did I have to travel before I'd realise I had gone too far? How much distance was enough?

I trembled as I wept. My hands shook and I could hardly see through the streaming tears. Nobody else would have noticed because I was *wandering* alone at some high speed on some busy road somewhere in Gauteng. If I think back carefully, I may have been on the R25 motorway opposite Greenstone Mall in Edenvale, but it could also have been anywhere. I can't remember exactly because during those many months of despair I covered hundreds of kilometres in my nomadic attempt at finding answers to my aching questions. *Where was I meant to be? Where was my place? Where should I work? Where was my home? Whom should I date? Where was he? What should my career be? Where should I live?* During those months I floated between one town and the next, gliding along the many motorways that joined the cities in the hope of finding the road or exit that connected me to the solution I was searching for.

A BURDEN LIFTING

Hear me when I call, O God of my righteousness!
You have relieved me in my distress; Have mercy
on me, and hear my prayer. – Psalm 4:1

That day was going no differently to any of the other days I had spent driving for kilometres in bewilderment with no clue where to go. But then something happened that had never taken place before. I had finally had enough and couldn't bare it any longer so amidst my blubbering mess of tears and bloodshot eyes, I finally screamed out to God - and He answered.

Just as I can still remember the way the shadows of the trees fell on the road I was on when I frantically cried out to God for help, I will never forget the precise feeling of what it felt like when I did. In a broken voice with howling tears streaming down my face, the second I screeched breathlessly, "Take these burdens from me God! Take them from me! They are not mine to bear! Take my burdens! I can't do this, I don't want them," a sudden real and tangible weight lifted upwards off from both of my shoulders.

The sensation was completely real and noticeable. It can best be likened to the instant relief you feel when you drop heavy parcels on the floor after carrying them for a long while and the strain is removed from your arms and fingers.

In that moment, the heaviness I had been carrying for the longest time suddenly vanished. The strangest thing is that the despondency and hopelessness within me had obviously been so great that it had manifested itself in a physical way. I did not know this was possible, and I also did not think that the depressing burden of confusion I was carrying would be released in the form of 'weights from my shoulders'. Why the relief came in the form of pressure being lifted from my shoulders, I am not certain, but that is how it came. The experience that day in the car was supernatural because what occurred wasn't visible to the naked eye but it was so obvious and clear to me.

In the dark hole I had gradually buried myself in, I saw no other way. Nothing else was working than to call out to God. In my weak and desperate plea for help, He answered. I wasn't even living a holy and righteous life that it would seem understandable for God to react immediately, but for some unfathomable reason He heard me. To this day I will never forget the feeling of that answer to a prayer, well in my case, a hysterical and frantic scream for help. So, without any doubt in my heart and mind, I know that God is there – always.

The LORD *is* near to all who call upon Him,
To all who call upon Him in truth.
He will fulfil the desire of those who fear Him;
He also will hear their cry and save them. – Psalm 145:18-19

When I cried out to Heaven I wasn't sitting in a church or praying with a minister or reading the Bible, I was in a tinny car on a bustling road in the middle of a busy city. Which goes to show, no matter where you are in your life and no matter what you are doing and no matter who you think you are, God is always there. It's your spirit that God sees, not your flesh. It is not your geographical location that He considers, it is your heart. If I think back now to the immediate events following my *burden lifting,* I can't remember any profound changes to my state of living during those dreadful months but I am definitely certain of one thing. If it wasn't for the Lord I wouldn't be sitting where I am today. That day was a milestone in my faith. In that moment so much was cemented for me.

And it shall come to pass in that day,
that his burden shall be taken away from off
thy shoulder, and his yoke from off thy
neck, and the yoke shall be destroyed because of the anointing.
- Isaiah 10:27

STRESS

During those long months of gloom, I had scratched my forearms until scabs formed. My existing skin condition of eczema flared up especially during this awful time due to the stress I was suffering. Anyone who has experienced eczema before knows that the inflamed area turns itchy which is then followed by the incessant need to scratch. I felt so terribly low during those long months that scraping away skin with my nails was only befitting to the trauma I was feeling. I had no idea where I was heading in my studies or where I was supposed to be living. The stress had just multiplied.

Stress is our body's way of responding to demands or threats. In my case, I often felt both. Because I lived all over Gauteng, already a province with exorbitant crime rates. Most of the places I stayed in were chosen because of the cheap cost of the rent, safety in these questionable areas was always an issue. There was many a night when I would drive around the block several times for fear of being cornered by a mysterious lingering vehicle.

On one too many occasions at the cockroach-infested-commune I lived at in Bryanston, the electric gate-motor stopped working. I was then forced to climb out of my car on a badly lit road to slide open the large black steel gate by myself. It was the only house on the street where the streetlights didn't work and so it was difficult to see if there was anyone lurking about. Because the landlord did not live on the property and had employed a ditsy dance instructor (a man more interested in doing the tango then improving the security) to run the commune, the entire driveway and front garden fell into darkness at night. Not one light around the outside of the house worked, so one was forced to use their phone light to find the doorstep. But if your phone battery was dead, perhaps the moonlight. Too bad if that night was overcast, or there was no full moon out. Any criminal could have easily slipped in through the unlocked gate, hid beneath the thick foliage and assaulted anyone in the driveway. Even if you got the chance to scream for help, no one inside the house would have flinched because the property was so huge and everyone just kept to themselves anyway.

I was so embarrassed about living there that I avoided inviting my friends over to visit. If I was being picked up or dropped off, I would meet them in the road and then quickly jump in the car as if part of a getaway. It sounds quite ridiculous that I allowed myself to live like this and under constant threat. *Why did I do it? Why would I knowingly test circumstances? Why would I put myself in a vulnerable position to be harmed? Why would I be so careless and so reckless? I knew the crime stats and was very aware of the lawlessness. Why was I not as concerned as I should have been?* How did I then repeatedly escape harm throughout these years? It amazes me how I was continually unscathed. *What was protecting me? Why was I so untouched?*

For He shall give His angels charge over you,
To keep you in all your ways. – Psalm 91:11

When I bought the Chevy, one of the first things I did was ask for God's hedge of protection over the vehicle. I asked for every driver and passenger to remain safe, as well as for His angels to protect me from harm. I lay over the car with my body and prayed for God's angels to have charge over the car. Until the moment I sold the car, not one person was injured in that vehicle. Across the thousands and thousands of kilometres travelled, through the great distances of country that was covered, throughout the night, the rain, the busy motorways and secluded side roads – every single person remained safe in that little orange Chevy Spark of mine. The Lord's gracious protection is what kept me and the other passengers safe from harm. I feel that God in His infinite wisdom and mercy allowed me this *period of grace* through which to journey through safely so that I could become the messenger He needed me to be. Without this journey of discovery, I may never have written this book that would tell of my *personal testimony of discovering the Truth*. Without this grace where would I be?

HARMFUL DISGUISES

The *fabrication* I was living demanded plenty of disguising and juggling from my side. Even though positive stress can sometimes be useful in achieving goals, this kind of stress wasn't. When stress is within your comfort zone, it can help you to stay focused and alert. But when the stress is beyond your reach, it stops being helpful and causes physical and mental damage. If I had continued allowing the negative stress to build up inside of me, I would have cracked in a way I shudder to imagine.

When managing stress, one of the most effective tools to alleviating the pressurising burden, is simply to talk about it. Talking is considered to be cathartic, and with my limited knowledge in this area of psychology, cathartic is defined as "providing relief through the open expression of strong emotion; causing catharsis". Catharsis is then the therapeutic feeling of being purified or being purged (removed) of something.

The benefits of verbally expressing emotions are numerous. The 'talking cure' is a technique that has become an important part of psychotherapy. Writing, talking or crying about negative events or feelings is a form of emotional disclosure.

Talking provides an immediate outlet of emotional release because when you share your worries and concerns, a sense of 'unloading' is experienced. Until I had experienced it first-hand, I never understood the impact of talking it out.

Talking eases isolation. By dropping the mask and being honest when opening up, the feeling that you are the only one experiencing what you're feeling is squashed. It can be very detaching when you think that you are the only one suffering through a particular issue or have ever suffered through anything. Most often than not, when you talk about your feelings, you realise that you are not the only person battling through something.

Talking also opens the lines for useful advice. The correctly informed person can offer you valuable insight into your problem and help you formulate a way forward to sorting out the complications you face. However, in order for an effective plan to be executed, you must be open and honest about the facts and your feelings. Holding back information won't help you.

Unfortunately, in my case. None of this worked back then. It could have, but it didn't because I wasn't talking at all. I wasn't talking to anyone, so no one could have helped anyway. Something was stopping me. No human knew a thing of what I was going through. I was wearing a disguise, and I'll tell you why.

FAKE IT 'TIL YOU MAKE IT

The human body reveals or projects invisible emotions and thoughts into a physical visible state. Mine periodically projected signs of inner confusion. I think it's the body's way of communicating what's taking place inside. Not only did I start smoking cigarettes at the age of twenty-three to kind of numb my confusion in a way (when I had always been dead-against-smoking), but my eczema also flared up.

A large portion of the stress I carried 'on my shoulders' was because I never let on about any of my stress. I never talked about it, I never spoke about it, and never hinted at it. I just plainly lied about the reality of my situation. No one ever suspected me of suffering through the agonising strain of confusion. Keeping it a secret also added to the weight of the burden in a massive way, making it heavier and more tiring to carry as the lies built up. It is taxing enough to endure stress, but not being *allowed* to speak about it, is very harmful. *You're probably wondering why I wasn't allowed to speak about it.* Because I wouldn't allow myself to speak about it. I simply couldn't bare the shame.

If anyone: friends, family members, colleagues and parents asked how I was doing, I would crack a crooked grin and mumble, "fine". This famous phrase carried me through those years of despair and saved me many times from the cringing experience of trying to explain what was really going on. "Fine" was sufficient. It worked. And then after delivering my "fine" and false smile ensemble, I would slink away into the crowd, avoiding chit-chat wherever I could. "Fine" was a good way to end the inevitable convo about my pitiful situation. Relationship, career, life plan, I was rock bottom. After years of practise, I had mastered the trick of changing the topic from my career to global warming, from relationships to politics, from where I was living to the Olympics, shifting the focus from me to anything else. This tool was useful. At all costs my awful reality had to be protected, no one was allowed to know. Especially not anyone I knew.

It's scary what a smile can hide.

As a result of this on-going cover up, I gradually lost confidence in myself. I was slowly dying inside. At one point I was so troubled, I longed to just mutter even one word of how I was feeling. I would even imagine approaching random strangers at the mall or in the parking lot just to hear myself speak the words out aloud. It would have been the smallest cry for support, but to give air to the words scratching to be released would help them escape. In my desperation I considered discussing my deep concerns with total strangers, who knew, perhaps the lady pushing the trolley up the ramp at the mall had the answers to my life's burning questions? Where should I go from here? Where are you going when you leave the mall? I would imagine asking them. Where do you think I should live and where's the best place to meet the people who will help me get to where I am meant to be? How long have you been living where you're living? Are you renting or did you buy? What are you doing with your life because I might need to consider that option? Where do you think I should go when I leave the mall? How do you spend your money? What is the best plan to live by and which one are you following because you look like you've got it all worked out? Do you perhaps know what my purpose is? Do you know of someone who can help me?

Now obviously I didn't ask random shoppers any of these questions, I wasn't a complete loon. But I was desperate enough to entertain the idea.

Picture this comical scenario: I run towards a vehicle waiting at the traffic light and knock on the window. The driver jolts with fright, scrunching their nose in annoyance. I then signal for them to roll down their car window so they can hear me ask my out-of-breath questions. *At this point I am certain they're riding their clutch to prepare for a quick getaway.* With barely a crack in the window I blurt out: "Hi, I am so sorry to bother you," in my sweetest voice. "Um, do you perhaps know what I should be doing with my life at the moment, more specifically which career path should I take?" A second later, off they speed while glaring at me in the revue mirror leaving me stranded still without any answers. A perfect analogy of how I felt back then, stranded and wondering where to turn.

If not for this reason alone, I knew one day I would write this book. Perhaps even to provide an explanation to the many people who were left baffled at my bizarre behaviour and thinking.

And … it seems to have all started with adolescence.

MY GRUELLING ADOLESCENCE

Adolescence: a fireworks display of confusion

After high school I became a master of disguises. A genius at faking it. I produced the sunglasses and pouting lips with the corporate clothing I wore to present an image of success. I donned the high heels with the short skirts to flaunt the seduction of the rat race. I highlighted the job satisfaction and idealised career plan I had regurgitated time and time again. I dollied up the progress I was making in my legal studies and the esteemed position I filled at the law firm. It was all a pretence in trying to conceal how I really felt about my disappointing self. The licence plates on my car might as well have spelled out, "Fake it 'til you make it".

I never once told anybody the real dilemma I was in. I had glittered and garnished my resume/CV to such an extent that I even included achievements from primary school because I hadn't achieved anything since grade twelve besides the few subjects at university. Even then, my matric results were disappointingly low because I disliked the last three years of high school so much. I never felt fully *present* at my second-high school, even though I developed wonderful friendships. I hardly studied and it showed, and now I have a lifelong hard copy in black and white to prove how miserable I was.

My academic results took a dismal plunge from the eighties to the fifties and sixties after I moved from one high school to another in grade ten. I remained at that percentile right through to the grade twelve final exams, simply because I had lost interest in myself. From being a top achieving straight A student throughout primary school and first two years of high school, to just getting by. I felt as if I was now floating in a reflectionless bubble of blasé. I no longer recognised myself. I was so unperturbed during those last three years of high school that the night before my grade twelve preliminary science exam, I stayed up until the early hours of the morning watching the 9/11 World Trade Centre saga unfold instead of studying. I was more interested with the *leaders of the free world* being under attack than the periodic table. It is still concerning though how unphased I was at the possibility of failing science, thankfully I didn't.

In another example of this uncharacteristic laidback and careless behaviour, I even managed to find my negligence amusing. This time it was during geography class. Part of our results in grade twelve were comprised of a portfolio made up of various assignments, of which I barely completed. Even though this portfolio counted for a large percentage of our year mark, I laughed it off and snickered when I received a miserable forty something percent at the end. "Oh, maybe I should have worked harder," were my half-hearted words as the teacher glared down at me after dropping the marked assignment on my table. The strange thing was that this attitude was so far from the girl I knew and once was. I was never the slacker and always the first in line to sign up. The one asking the questions and the one trying to answer them as well. I was used to achieving within the top three percentages in the class, which ranged anything between eighty to ninety percent. I was used to playing sport and being selected for teams. I was used to being eager to participate in any cultural event at school and doing more than what was required of me. Now as an adolescent, I couldn't think of anything worse. I would stare at my feet and shuffle away behind one of the taller girls if the teacher even appeared to be glancing in my direction. This unfamiliar behaviour and thoughtless attitude that had developed was so shocking to me. I felt helpless because it felt like I was walking someone else's path, and didn't I know what to do. I couldn't escape my own body or redo these three miserable years – what could I possibly do? I was so confused. I didn't know who this adolescent person was. *What had happened? What had changed in me?*

I knew who the child in me was: happy, well-balanced, and full of confidence. But this version, I did not know at all. So, in my last feeble attempt at providing a plausible excuse for my ridiculous geography portfolio result and all the other abnormal behaviour I exhibited, I conjured up a reason, "I couldn't be blamed, because it wasn't me. This was not the real me. I wasn't fully aware of the weight of the assignment and how much it would impact my final results for the subject, so I was off the hook. I wasn't really engaged, so I couldn't be blamed." *I wanted to reject and ignore who this version of me was, so I was allowed to think and act bizarrely.*

**If you spend your time being someone else,
who will spend their time being you?**

To illustrate the depth of my detachment I felt during those bleak adolescent years, I'll share a memory that expresses how much I wanted to escape who I was. When walking from one classroom to the next at school, I would go out of my way to walk in the shade of the building or in the shade of the trees. This way nobody would be able to see me.

I didn't want to be noticed by anyone. I had accidently become someone I didn't know.

Why had this happened? Why had I become like this? What had changed?

**One of the worst moments in someone's life is when
they're watching their whole world fall apart before
their eyes, and all they can do is stare blankly.**

When putting my resume/CV together, I would only reveal the one distinction I received for art and not any of the other subject marks because they too obviously reflected the lack of effort on my part. These poor results not only displayed my gloomy state of mind but also the severe distance I now had from my former self. The Candace I once knew was missing during the second half of high school and had been replaced with a girl I didn't recognise. The confident and energetic achiever was now withdrawn. The participating go-getter was missing and all I was left with now was shame. *How had I become like this? Who was this person dodging every opportunity to be a part of something? Why was this happening to me? Everyone else seemed so involved and unrestricted. Everyone else seemed so eager to jump aboard this adolescent train.*

Anguish: gazing into a mirror and there's no recognisable reflection.

The blatant contrast between who I was once was and who I was supposed to be, was like night and day. The people I bumped into whom I knew before grade ten barely recognised me. Not only had I added thirty kilograms to the scale but the self-assured winner had disappeared. A nasty cycle had emerged and was clearly visible to everyone. When one is uncharacteristically overweight, your energy levels drop along with your motivation to exercise. So being reluctant to exercise, coupled with a lack in energy does nothing to decrease your expanding waistline which in turn depletes your motivation to decrease it. It's a vicious cycle. Anyone who knows anything about struggling with weight gain will know how it feels to continuously face your enemies wherever you go. You're always at war with the mirror. And not just your home mirror but also the reflection in the bank window, shop windows, photographs, the scale, food, the beach, second helpings, changing rooms, clothing shops, portion control, fellow diners, self-control, eating out, the gym, and exercising. Knowing when the war began will always be planted firmly in my memory. The moment the physical change had become an issue, was the moment I changed over from the energetic bag of fun to the plump girl hiding in the corner.

THE BOSSY PHYSICS OF PUBERTY

The cool August breeze didn't stop us. We were fifteen-and-a-half and only in grade nine so swimming was a fun thing to do. Oblivious to anything other than the water, my friend and I jumped in and out of the pool all afternoon just enjoying what kids normally do. It was during one of these intermissions between diving and climbing out that I sat down on a nearby step to rest when I noticed something I had never seen before. In the dimming light of the autumn afternoon, I saw my bear thigh. Never before in all my childhood years had I ever considered my upper leg in such a way. Uncovered in broad daylight, it suddenly seemed wrong to have it exposed like that. Suddenly I became aware of it from a young women's perspective and no longer a young girl's. *What was this change in me?*

I also noted how its contour had changed: from straight to more curved. I had never before inspected it with such scrutiny. And then it dawned on me: my body was changing. It was growing up and was ready for the next phase of life: adolescence. Without me knowing it, without me giving it permission to do so, it had moved to the next phase. This was impossible. I had not given it permission to do so. I wasn't ready to move on. I wasn't ready not to be carefree. Whose thigh was this that glared back at me? I had not permitted this change yet. Not only was my leg curvier but also fuller, as opposed to the skinny childlike one I grew up with and was used to.

To this day I will never forget that moment at the pool where I came face-to-face with realising that things would no longer be the same. There was no going back. Worst of all, I wasn't ready for it. That moment was so significant I still remember what we ate for lunch that day next to the pool - *Mince Mate* (a pasta dish with saucy mince). My body had stepped onto the escalator going up and was heading for the second floor but my mind and heart still lingered at the bottom being shoved from all sides by others trying to hop on. I was not ready to hop on yet.

From that day on I became conscious of how my body moved and reacted, in contrast to primary school where I was nonchalant and happy-go-lucky. I became aware of how it reacted to differing factors like particular fits of clothing, colours, exercise, and food consumption. In turn developing an awareness of how I perceived it. Life had closed a door to one chapter, and even though I could peek through the window into the room I once lived in, there was no way I could return. If I was desperate enough, I could try and re-enter and live their once more, but in all honesty, how could I? *Why would I want to delay moving on to the next phase? Why would I want to remain being a child, when I wasn't one anymore? I couldn't possibly do that to myself.* I knew what waited back there, childhood and naivety, innocence and carefreeness, but I had to move on and forward, for my sake. There was no other choice. Unfortunately, this was easier said than done because my mind wouldn't budge from its drifting position at the bottom of the escalator, even though it sent my body to do the work of growing up. For the next five years my head remained dangling at the bottom of those revolving stairs, leaving me disconnected with a feeling of separateness. *No wonder why, I was walking without my brain.*

Cracked mirror = warped reflection

Once you're aboard the fast-moving train heading for the next section of your life, it's really impossible to climb off. The best decision is: make the most of your journey. However, shortly after my smack-in-the-face-with-reality that day at the pool, I moved from one high school to the next. Traumatic as this is to many who seem to cope just fine, I didn't. It was these last three years of high school where I found myself wanting to escape who I had become. Remembering that my mind was still back in the old body I used to have, not in this foreign one I barely recognised.

Along with being bussed to a new school at the impressionable age of fifteen without feeling fully *connected,* I started picking up body weight in response to this overwhelming sense of detachment. There I was at the beginning of the school year, at a new school in a new city with awkward feelings of disassociation and a growing weight issue. *Not a good solution for a weakening body image and declining self-esteem I'd say.*

Females generally have higher levels of body discontent than men. Media plays a large role in this.

BODY IMAGE

Body image is the picture you form in your mind about the appearance of your body, including how you perceive others to see your body. The mental picture we form about our body can be completely different to the actual appearance of it. How we identify with our physical self, alters the thoughts and feelings that result from this identification. These thoughts and feelings can be positive or negative and can be influenced by various factors.

In my case, a negative body image developed the moment I grasped the fact that my body was changing and there was nothing I could do to stop the process. I found myself in a situation in which I had lost total control. Psychologically speaking, I am sure one could attribute several conditions using this outline of how I felt, but in simple terms, I felt torn. Torn between the childhood happy-go-lucky physical way I experienced life: with me running innocently on the front lawn to performing on stage in front of the entire school in costume, from playing wildly in the pool for the whole day with friends to jumping on the trampoline in a bathing suit and having no qualm with the world, then all the way to this foreign physical state I found myself in.

The *child body* I grew up with, I knew how it worked, how it ran, how it jumped, how it swam, how it danced, caught the sun, played, pained, ached, somersaulted, did handstands and sprang. I was confident, self-assured, bubbly, talkative, interested, participative, achieving, well-balanced and full of optimism about the future that lay ahead. I was present and had dreams and aspirations. But this all dissolved when I saw that it had changed right before my eyes. I didn't know how to react. My mind felt separate from my body so I developed a distorted perception of my actual appearance: i.e., my reality.

There were many times where I considered myself the fat girl but afterwards discovered that my friends really didn't have this perception of me at all. I had created this reality where I was the useless, overweight ugly one in the corner who didn't deserve to be treated fairly.

A negative body image can also involve a warped perception of size and shape, as well as more general feelings of shame, awkwardness and anxiety about one's body. People with a negative body image tend to feel that their size and shape are signs of personal failure and reflects their worth. In my eyes, I had failed myself because I had failed physically. I was not the person I once was and definitely not the person I wanted to be and thought I would be. From this point on all areas suffered and so I slowly withdrew from being part of my own life.

Dale: "She's put on so much weight since the last time I saw her."
Sarah: "Have you seen how much weight she has put on?"
Donna: "All my weight goes to my thighs. I look like a hippo."
Claire: "I've put on weight again. I just hate
the way my arms look when I am fat."

Since that day at the pool, *the relationship with my own body* became destructive and so the next five or so years were spent wrestling this harmful connection. The chilling awareness that my body had taken on its natural progression into puberty without my consent sparked a ripple effect into thinking that any other factor that has the ability to influence my body should be treated in contempt and so an adverse association to food was triggered.

Food had become an enemy because I no longer had the same relationship I previously had with it: untroubled and of no consequence. An awareness of something that wasn't an issue before had now emerged and it showed in the way I contemplated meal times, as if they were public speaking engagements. As mealtimes grew closer, my anxiety grew because I knew what lay ahead. The agonising analysis of the food placed before me, and with the weighing up of how each ingredient would influence my body. I could no longer identify with a meal as I did before. Where I once was more interested in leaving the table to climb a tree than sit and eat, I was now considering calories and portion sizes, or whether there was butter in the pumpkin or not, or whether the extra pork chop was big enough, or whether anyone noticed me dishing up extra rice or going back for seconds. My previous positive association with healthy sustenance had disappeared along with my childhood body.

Where I used to eat a right sized portion knowing that the more one ate, the more one stretched their stomach which then needed more food the next mealtime to feel satisfied, I was now sneaking in seconds and thirds before and after meals. The internal battle became consuming. All my knowledge of staying slim had subconsciously escaped my adolescent brain and was switched with the dog-in-a-chicken-coop-effect - bombardment when faced with too much free range. Trying to control my intake of food triggered an overshadowing obsession with it, so I became hooked to having negative feelings towards it. The child was gone and I was left with an adolescent who now had to *watch* what she ate because calories were no longer shed with running and playing outside, they were shed by actively watching them. So, from the age of fifteen-and-a-half until twenty-one years old, mealtimes were deemed obstacles because I had to endure the agony of tackling this horrible habit.

Living in a skin you don't feel comfortable in is like hiding from your shadow. For at least six years I lived and breathed inside a body I didn't recognise and battled to accept. Our physical self is an integral part of our human condition and so how one connects with this integral part will like ripples in a pond effect other areas of who one is. This is but one example of how I know we exist in both flesh and spirit. My spirit had been damaged because of the damage to my body image and my negative body image affected my spirit, causing a cycle of inner turmoil.

EMBARRASSING FOOD EPISODES

Even after I finished high school and started attending university, my overbearing obsession came with me. It got so bad that one day I walked down to the on-campus food store to buy five caramel/chocolate covered donuts. I knew as soon as I ordered the baked goods I shouldn't have done so. It felt wrong and I felt guilty. While standing at the till to pay, holding onto the big white box in my hand with the five seductive donuts inside, I felt like I was smuggling contraband. In that moment I had built my very own obstacle that required tackling. *Why would I do this to myself? Why? It's like I wanted to create more resentment for myself?* I knew I had issues with self-control when it came to food. *Why would I actively self-sabotage myself like this and set myself up for torture?* It was like a drug. A drug that made me squirm in self-pity and self-loathing. I guess I did it because I despised who I was. Deep down I wanted to punish my body for letting me down and transforming without my consent. I was supposed to avoid situations like these. I was supposed to be smart with the *addiction to these negative feelings,* but fell to pieces at the site of the donuts and listened to that destructive voice inside my head. "Yum, they look good enough to lead you down a path of skin-crawling torment." *Sure, I'll take five.*

It gets worse. The shame of it.

Gasp … and this is embarrassing.

Upon leaving the store I made my way through the masses of happily chatting students and headed straight for the ladies' toilet. Picked a cubicle and closed the door. I then carefully sat down on the closed toilet seat and opened the box. Staring back at me were five perfectly round juicy donuts calling out my name, tempting me like a snake charmer. My hands quivered and my heartbeat picked up pace. *The voices* in my head were spitting at each other and arguing for attention. And then it happened, *'the self'* caved and I took hold of one of the donuts and bit into it, right there on the toilet seat in a busy university bathroom.

The first bite was followed by a second and then quickly a third and soon the first donut was gone. Like a bickering troubled couple arguing across my shoulders, *the voices* of reason and guilt bounced across my head but I kept at it. I then ignored the nudge to stop as I started on the second donut. Through each bite the battle continued. I felt helpless because I just couldn't help myself out of this moment. *Should I stop eating now? Are you really going to eat five donuts here in the loo? You seriously don't need to eat all five. Should I stop eating now … or now … or now. But you've already eaten two, what's one more? You might as well just go for them all. Just get up and stop with this stupidity Candace. Shame on you, who does this? What will the other people outside the cubicle think of you if they found out? This is beneath you, isn't it?* Shame knows no shame, I guess. Five donuts later I was done and had packed on enough self-loathing for the coming week. I was good to go.

If I wasn't alienated enough, this was one way to really establish distance: hiding to eat in secret.

Body dissatisfaction is a threat to your well-being.

The university accommodation I boarded in consisted of eight single bedrooms on each floor of the ten two storey buildings. Most of us had our own fridges and microwaves in which to cook and were responsible for the cooking of our own meals. Midway through my second year, one of the new members to our residence of ladies asked me whether I could store her large bag of fish fingers in my fridge freezer which I happily agreed to do. The first few days they went unnoticed but after a week or so the *addictive need* scratched its way out and I tore open the heavy-duty plastic bag filled with fish fingers. These fish fingers were obviously a bulk buy from the rejected section of an established meat factory because each finger was either misshapen or shorter than your average supermarket kind but with the same taste and consistency. As I placed a couple on my plate to cook in the microwave, I undertook to replace each and every one. Two weeks later the entire contents of the bag needed replacing. I had gradually eaten all of this trusting girl's fish fingers of which I quickly enquired whether I could eat a few in the hope she would just say she had forgotten about the storage arrangement, but she hadn't. I was fortunate for her understanding and for her lack in interest regarding the fish-finger-guzzling-episode. Considering the type of girl she was, she was far more interested in being charmed by men whereas I was sadly more concerned with being charmed by fish.

More people would overcome their shortcomings and failures, if they weren't so busy denying them.

Because I had developed a negative relationship with food, I became obsessed with its uncontrollable hold on me. I remember waking my friend up early one morning at the residence to give me the homemade muesli she had granted me the night before. Even though she was obviously sleeping at the time, I knocked incessantly on her door at 8am that morning but it didn't bother me. I just had to have some of that nutritional mix she spoke of. Little did I remember that if you have three bowls of nutritional muesli at breakfast, it loses its nutritional value and turns into ... fat. Too much of anything is a bad thing. *It was almost as if I had developed this bad eating habit on purpose.*

Being right in the middle means you can't see from the outside what the situation needs.

Another pathetic example of my weird relationship to food was evident when my university friends and I ate out at McDonalds, but I would bring along a yogurt instead. Everyone else tucked into their tasty chips and nuggets while I sat there like a glutton spooning my full cream yogurt under the illusion that burgers and fries were the enemy and not a tub of double thick full cream chocolate yogurt. I naively thought that everyone avoided the fast food of McDonald's because it was 'supposedly fattening and disastrous to your waistline' but later realised that it really isn't about eating the occasional burger and fries that causes weight gain, it is the regular overindulgence of this kind of food without any exercise that is the problem. Can you see how crazily I isolated myself? There is nothing wrong with eating a juicy burger and salty fries from one of your favourite fast-food outlets once in a while, going overboard by bringing your own spoon and yogurt is.

Why was I doing this? Why would I try and isolate myself on purpose?

My battle at this post high school stage was really about being disconnected from the person who I thought I would have been at this point. It really all began when I noticed the unconsented change in my body at the end of grade nine. This resulted in a huge weight gain at the beginning of grade ten which left me unrecognisable to myself causing me to withdraw because I no longer felt comfortable in my own skin. I really didn't connect with the person who I now was which is why I backed out of events, appointments and activities. I no longer participated as I did before. I simply wasn't doing my life. During those five to six years after grade ten, *my life was a blur.*

NEEDING TO BE READY TO WRITE THIS FINAL DRAFT

And whoever exalts himself will be humbled, and he who humbles himself will be exalted.
- Matthew 23:12

I mentioned in the introduction that I always knew I would write this book. I just felt it all along. All throughout my *decade of despair* I felt that one day I would write all of it down and share it so that others could benefit from it. From the point where I slipped into my *blurry bubble* in grade ten at sixteen-years-old to about the age of twenty-six, I frequently felt there was no way I was going through all of this agonizing confusion for nothing. I was convinced that none of it was happening in vain. There was definitely a greater purpose taking place amidst the heartache and blank perplexity. But at the same time, I also knew that I couldn't write it unless I was brutally honest. In order to disclose the *whole truth,* I would have to be vulnerable. This means exposing my shortcomings. I would have to divulge my insecurities and faults for all to read. In order for the story to be credible in its entirety, being used specifically for the purpose of benefitting and helping others, I would have to open up about my weaknesses so that others would believe me when I shared about how I had changed and grown. Nobody willingly seeks criticism and judgment from anybody, so by admitting my faults and failures on paper I risk facing attack and ridicule. But if I can help others, then it's worth it. If I can point others towards *the light,* then it's all worth it. At the heart of it, I want to help others.

Only in hindsight can I comprehend why I had to journey through this decade of unrhythmic misplacement. It's because I had to break in order to be built up. In my brokenness I cried out to God for help. In my brokenness I realised I couldn't do life without His guidance. In my brokenness I was being humbled. I felt so out of place in the places I was searching for answers, that I had no other option than to look for what God wanted from me. Maybe I was not the problem solver, maybe He was. Where I had been searching was hopeless, they were dead ends.

I needed to jump aboard His plan for my life, instead of my own because it clearly wasn't working. It was in my brokenness that He heard my cries and answered my desperate prayers. So, from the moment in grade nine when I first became unrecognisable to myself to roughly the age of twenty-six, a tremendous amount happened to shape me into the person I am today. Shaping me to be the messenger I am today. Going through it was hideously difficult but coming out victoriously is wonderfully life-giving. From my disgraceful food episodes, to trying to escape my reflection. From my bad choice in transport, to my pursuit in a lifeless career. From my thwarted attempts at various jobs, to my low self-body image. From wrestling with relationships to multiple disappointments, I had ultimately been moving against God's rhythm for my life, and it was His rhythm I needed to find. That's actually what I was searching for.

I am therefore humbling myself and lay bare my failures in order for the truth to be revealed. In these pages I hope to share what is real - *the good, the bad and the ugly* - so that others may come to see what I have seen and learn from what I have learnt. I also mention in the first few pages of this book (the one you're physically reading now) that this is the third attempt at this story. The first two contracted a virus known as 'writers block' and killed themselves off rather quickly. The second book's case of 'writers block' was so severe that I didn't even make it to page two. I am so thankful because both versions would have painted me as a ridiculous attention seeker and done nothing for the glory of God. The glory would have been mine, with a flashy title and gold lettering, I would have showcased only *the good* and none of the *bad* or the *ugly*. I am certain that God intervened in cutting those attempts right at the start because I really would have wasted my time. The writings would have been pointless, embarrassing actually.

I felt that in His infinite wisdom, God knew the final version wasn't ready to be written, because I wasn't ready. My two pathetic attempts of sharing what I thought others needed to hear about my journey were obliterated. I needed to be fuller in my spiritual walk with the Lord before I could share what needed to be shared. My eyes needed to be *fully* opened in order for me to show others what I had seen because during the first two attempts they most definitely were not.

I only see this now: after-the-fact. Even up until two months before I officially sat down to attempt writing the third draft, I still wasn't ready ... and then something happened during these two months which would lay the foundation for and later construct this book entirely.

I still have many things to say to you, but you cannot bear *them* now. However, when He, the Spirit of truth has come, He will guide you into all truth; for He will not speak on His own *authority*, but whatever He hears He will speak; and He will tell you things to come. He will glorify Me, for He will take of what is Mine and declare *it* to you. All things that the Father has are Mine. Therefore I said that He will take of Mine and declare *it* to you. – John 16:13

All those years I thought about writing the book were years in preparation, but I was still not completely ready because I had not seen what I needed to see in order for the real message to be revealed.

Two months before my final semester exams, I experienced the most intense life changing *revelation* I could have ever imagined being humanly possible. It was such a spectacular spiritual experience that it gave me the most colossal indescribable clarity thinkable. I saw into the depths of another realm of understanding. This perspective shifting, *outer-planetary* metamorphic experience impacted me so greatly that my life is forever changed.

I had no choice but to plead for grace for my upcoming exam period because after this experience I became so mesmerised with what I had been shown that all I wanted to do was soak up God's Word. The quandary was I had to focus on my studies. During these two months I became so hungry for Scripture and Biblical teaching that all I wanted to do was soak it up as much as possible. The Lord did grant me grace and even delivered me through a terrible examination that without His outpouring of peace I would not have made it through and would have had to rewrite it. I figure that God wanted me to be done with the studying so that I could focus on the writing of this book during those six months after my exams and that is why he delivered me through that time.

Since my early twenties, this book has been burning inside to be documented. But I needed the right wisdom, knowledge, character and time to tackle it. Which meant the six months from June to December 2016, after my course was done, was crucial in getting most of the content written. So that is exactly what happened. I received *my magnificently special awakening during those two to three months, I'll call it 'my unveiling'*, wrote and passed my exams and then started on the content of this book. But this time from the right perspective. I would have needed to be finished with my studies to fully focus on this message. God's timing was so perfect, only He knew!

I must honestly say that during the writing of the third attempt of this book, the one in which I needed to have been fully ready to write, I haven't experienced one word of writer's block. Not one moment. Nothing.

I have not once battled with what to write as each sentence has flowed seamlessly. Each word has simply melted from my fingertips onto the page, with sentences gently blending into paragraphs as if they were streaming onto the screen. It actually feels as if the book has written itself and I was merely the typist who captured the words given to me. I have been led from the choice in title to the arrangement of the chapters, as well as from which topic to deal with first to the content of each subdivision. *I am amazed.*

It is difficult to explain 'being led by God' in a world where many haven't acknowledged the presence and power of the Holy Spirit and He's hand in a servant's journey. To say that the Holy Spirit has guided this book, by: prompting every sentence, connecting the flow from one to the next which in turn formed balanced paragraphs, arranging every memory into a sequence befitting of an understandable layout, is overwhelmingly bold. *How could I possibly say this? But this is exactly how it felt. From not being able to write even one page in two other separate attempts, to writing almost two-hundred-and-fifty pages. Wow! I must have had help.*

But the Helper, the Holy Spirit, whom the Father will send in My name, He will teach you all things, and bring to your remembrance all things that I said to you. – John 14:26

Even before I officially started with page one, I had before me over fifteen topics I wished to write on as well as all the research and ideas mixed-up together in a folder that looked like an organised mess. I had no clue where to begin. How was I ever going to select and categorise all the material I had collected into coherent meaningful sentences, let alone chapters? I had never done this before. This was my first time setting out to finish writing a book. I needed a manual for writing a testimony, I needed guidance. There was no way I could do this by myself and there was no glimmer of a plan developing anywhere. I was lost and I needed help … then I prayed.

I prayed for the first time ever before writing. I prayed to be led by the Holy Spirit as I was writing for the Lord Himself and needed His message to be revealed, not mine. And then I got specific. Because I had no clue of where to begin with this mountain of material I had collected or even what I needed to say, I asked the Lord to tell me where to start writing and on what topic I should begin with. I wanted the right message, His message to be shared. This time would be different because I was different. Something had happened to me, something colossal and it needed to be shared. I needed help though. There was no way I could do this alone.

No sooner had I uttered the words did the answer come flowing like running water into my being. The words were: "Pride" – start at pride. The first chapter must be about pride, because that is where it all began.

PART
ONE

PRIDE

For pride is spiritual cancer: it eats up the very
possibility of love, or contentment, or even
common sense. – CS Lewis, *Mere Christianity*

First area pride affected: career

And establish the work of our hands for us;
Yes, establish the work of our hands.
- Psalm 90:17

"Trusting the test and its answers" is a universal approach to reaching conclusions. This is why these words accurately introduce this section of the chapter on pride because I used to share the same sentiment. There were three areas during my *decade of disaster*, between the ages of fifteen-and-a-half and twenty-six, that were severely affected by pride and which ultimately caused much of my dismay. This is why we start at pride.

How does this sentiment then relate to me and my three main areas of self-destruction? I'll tell you. I was relying on man to give me the answers, and not God. I was relying on myself, my worldly desires, the aptitude tests, and Ally McBeal for career guidance.

Ally McBeal (1997 – 2002) was a legal comedy-drama television series that aired on South African television during the late nineties when I was about thirteen-years-old. For those of you who don't remember, or have never watched the series, the show was about a young female attorney working in the corporate world of a Boston law firm. She was particularly ditsy and very eccentric, yet talented and attractive. So, at the impressionable age of thirteen, I thought she was the perfect model of what to aspire to. Little did I know that this desire to emulate her was based only on what I could see through the television screen, in other words, a fabricated reality. She was simply made-up, a character.

Even though the story of my career ideals ultimately began with the fictional character of *Ally McBeal* and her imaginary dance partners, it really materialised once I had taken the mandatory aptitude tests at the beginning of my first year at university in 2002. Before the first semester commenced, all first-year students undertook aptitude testing to confirm that their chosen area of study was actually the best fit for them. And then I took mine …

BUCKLE YOUR SEATBEALTS, THIS IS GOING TO BE A BUMPY RIDE

Little did I know that the three-year undergraduate degree which I undertook to study would eventually turn into an academic voyage of fourteen-and-a-half years. I shake my head in disbelief just calculating the time difference of eleven-and-a-half years of extra study time. What's also amazing though, is how I managed to make it through the gruelling process alive. It was a tiresome undertaking that threw at me one trial after the next, leaving me dealing with despondency and hopelessness most of the time – a true test of endurance that's for sure. But I survived. I made it through so much torment that I am now ecstatic to call myself a survivor. Anyone who has gone through the same struggle, would surely understand what a test of strength of character it is.

As I sit here at my laptop reflecting on how I felt at my lowest and darkest moments. Where quitting any form of further study would have been way easier, I feel relieved that I endured through the many countless days, weeks and months of frustration and difficulty. The regrets of quitting would have torn me to pieces. I would have been bitter and regretful, spending each day after the decision to quit, in continual self-criticism. If I had given up on my goal of earning a degree at any stage during those tough years, I would have found myself in the exact same desperate position now as I was then - something I am thankful I had foresight into. I was able to overcome those carnal impulses of opting for the instant solution. The quick fix as they say. I was able to deny the desire of temporary comfort and look ahead into what my future might look like, as well as what it would look like if I I had given up. My failures and weaknesses didn't get the best of me. I didn't allow them to win. I endured through them and pushed through those tough times. I am now more aware than ever that I am strong enough to see something through to the end.

As I write these very words it has been four months since I graduated (June 2016). Even though I have now achieved the goal I had set out to achieve, the biggest reward wasn't that I was capped or obtained the degree, it is knowing that I was equipped to bare the hardship. I had it in me. The characteristics to help me endure. The characteristics of perseverance and endurance, surrendering, sacrifice and foresight. Being able to conquer and overcome the fear, the despondency, the frustration, the stress, the anger, the depression, the guilt, and the shame with much resilience, was without a doubt, God-given.

God heard me that day in my Chevy Spark while driving some ridiculous speed when I cried out to Him, sobbing in emotional pain, and has heard me ever since. This journey of discovering who I was, was more a journey of discovering who He is.

Adversity, if managed correctly, prepares ordinary people for a chance at real growth.

University aptitude tests were taken during our orientation (*ontgroening*) period. Orientation is something all first year students must go through to begin campus life. Since it is a rite of passage for those entering the domain of the more seasoned students, it is at the same time a rite of honour for the older students to do the initiating. The official period of initiation lasts for at least two weeks, and takes place between two and three weeks before the day students arrive for their first semester classes. This means the entire campus is mostly accessible for induction purposes, leaving the lecture halls open for drilling anthems and the cafeteria free for parading.

I am sure that initiation differs at various universities, but the one I was at, the grind took place 24/7. For those two-and-a-half weeks we were: deprived of sleep, constantly instructed and ordered about the whole day, renamed (*by naam*) with a 'house name' and which became the only name you were permitted to use, required to build the RAG float (*blommetjies vou* – of which I must have folded two thousand palm-sized plastic flowers), rehearsed for the first years play, deprived of more sleep, instructed to march, practised our house songs, socialised with other on-campus residences, danced (*sokkie*), serenaded (*serrie*), ran and hid from the house committee (*Haka*), rehearsed some more, sang, were woken up at all hours of the night for inspections, and finally amidst all this exhaustion took our aptitude tests.

During the test sessions, being the first years, we would all nap between sections of the test by resting on the table in front of us or by leaning on one another. During other evaluations, we'd lie on one another's legs and arms just to get that extra five minutes of shut-eye. We were exhausted during our initiation period. "Daar's nie eers tyd om te pee nie," commented one of my housemates during initiation. (Loosely translated: There isn't even time to use the loo.)

HITTING SNAGS

Snag #1: embarrassing timetable

I obtained entry into the university with being accepted to study a Bachelor of Arts in Marketing Communications but after reviewing my timetable during the first week of lectures, I noticed how embarrassingly sparse it looked. With classes dotted occasionally across the grid, I wondered where all my class time was. I immediately doubted two things: the point of me staying on campus which was costing my parents, and the worth of the degree I had chosen to study. Both of these factors caused doubt in my proposed career path and in myself.

I thought that my pitiful timetable was yet another confirmation of the pitiful sub-version I had become, an exercise that snowballed into a useless cycle of regret and self-doubt. It was in that moment that I remembered my aptitude test results. They would give me a way out of this situation and possibly save me. They would be a way for me to restore my former credibility and the primary school reputation I once had of someone who didn't take the easy road and obtained exceptionally high results. This sparse class schedule laying on my desk before me was a reflection of someone who had come to university to loaf around. *Or so I stupidly thought. Little did I know that Marketing Communications is actually one of the most ambitious career paths to pursue. Oh, how blindly proud I was. Its ugly face mocking me.*

I wanted to be that person who had chosen a *difficult* course to study because that person was known to be up for a challenge. A notion which meant I was smart. Since the test results indicated that my aptitude would be best served if I study one of the law degrees available: Bachelor of Commerce in Law, LLB Law or Bachelor of Arts in Law I would most likely make the right choice by choosing one of them. The options presented would save me from turning blood red with embarrassment when asked to show my timetable to others. With Law I could stand proud next to my peers even though none of them really cared what I was studying. This way I wouldn't feel ashamed of my choice in degree, my weight or my timetable. A Law degree would help me cover up some of my miserable mistakes and terrible high school track record. It would give me an opportunity to redeem myself.

I am better than this silly little Bachelor of Arts degree that any student who barely scraped through year twelve could do. I am better than this. I'll die of shame if I have to tell someone that I am only doing a Bachelor of Arts degree. Arts – how pitiful. I don't want other people to think that I'm studying 'B', 'A' for 'Bugger All'. I don't want to be classified on the same level as those 'other BA students', the ones who sit on the campus lawn all day long and smoke one cigarette after the next. This definitely didn't suit my reputation of being smart, I must do something worthy of my intellect. This silly BA degree would not make me successful and rich, only a Law degree would. It would be so humiliating to be poor one day, especially if I could have avoided it. People deem lawyers highly and consider them to be important, just like in Ally McBeal. I would much prefer being known as a Law student than a BA student. That's what I'll do, I'll swop over to an LLB Law and ditch this silly good-for-nothing degree.

The fear of man brings a snare, But whoever
trusts in the Lord shall be safe.
– Proverbs 29:25

Several months into making the initial switch I was passing all of my semester tests and exams and so was satisfied with how my academics were progressing. Part of this academic success was attributed to the close scrutiny and tight reins from our *Haka* (house committee) and house lady who kept us in check and out of usual university mischief. As first years we were given strict curfews and time slots in which to work. Study times were mandatory and under no circumstances, were we allowed to attend parties on and off campus, let alone even possess a car. These regulations imitated the ones I was naturally comfortable with so I had no problem fitting in with this.

Snag #2: instant unprepared freedom

The problem arose however in the second year when the rules vanished. No more curfews, no more mandatory study times and no more regulations. This meant I was instantly stranded and left spinning for the right direction in which to turn. The structures and authorities who once guided my every movement were all of a sudden just gone. This new way of doing things came as a shock to my system because I was now forced to manage my time and didn't know how to. I was lost once again! I had stumbled into unchartered territory and didn't have a clue on how to handle all this freedom. Before I had the safety net of boundaries and limits to catch me, but now I had nothing. I only had myself and it was far too overwhelming. This is when I slid into a negative downward spiral.

For the first time in my life, I could choose entirely what time to go to bed, what time to get up, what time to prepare food, when I was going to class, whether I would even attend class, whether I was going to a social event or not, and how late I was going to stay. With all this new-found uncharted freedom, things started changing. For the first few weeks I slept in and didn't even bother waking up to my alarm clock, even if it was set for me to get up for class. There were days where I didn't even put on fresh clothing. I simply threw on a baggy jacket over my pyjama top, climbed into a pair of crumpled up tracksuit pants lying on the floor and dragged my legs down to class twenty minutes before it started. These twenty minutes gave me enough time to sneak into the back row just as the lecture started and quickly exit as it ended.

The contrast to how the other students and I responded to getting the most from varsity life was so blatantly apparent that one would think we were breathing different forms of air. There were girls who were so motivated to make this varsity experience work for them that they dollied themselves up so much that they looked like celebrities, whereas I didn't even bother brushing my hair some days. Rolling the mess on my head into a ball and then clipping it up was enough for me. Some other girls simply looked nice and presentable because they just did what normal people do with their appearance, and put in some effort. I would have taken nice but I didn't have any inclination anymore. There were also students who looked so care free and content with being nineteen-years-old, whereas I was hiding inside my baggy clothes with the notion that covering up with baggier clothes was better. In my original plan, in the one I had dreamed of as a young girl while watching *Ally McBeal,* I would be a slim, attractive, well-dressed, well-balanced popular Law student with a nice boyfriend to match. Unfortunately, this dream of mine slipped through my fingers in the same way as my childhood body did, and there I was, stuck in a place inside a growing bubble. *What was wrong with me? Why couldn't I just be normal?* All I wanted for was to feel special like those other girls did when their boyfriends greeted them after a lecture, look pretty like they did, be liked and well-balanced like they were. *What was wrong with me? I just hated this version of me.*

Snag #3: wearing a big yellow repellent

But alas, my surrounding bubble had grown too thick now for anyone to notice me. Even inside this bubble with its gradually thickening layer of murky semi-translucent film, I battled to fully see out into the world. After months of squinting to even see my own face within the bubble's disappearing reflective surface, I could no longer make out who I was amidst the muffled noises that came from outside it. Within the entrapment of the bubble, my voice had also been muted. The voice that speaks out for help, for guidance, for anything. It had shut down and closed off access to any real feelings and expression. For fear of being shamed, coupled with too much pride in admitting my weaknesses and failures, I remained silent throughout those two years at university. I knew I had fixable issues and knew I needed help, but was too proud to admit it.

To make matters worse I distanced myself even more by wearing my oversized canary yellow house jacket everywhere I went. I didn't want others to see my body the way I perceived it, disgraceful and off-putting (to me at least). So, I tried covering its imperfections up by wearing a bulky jacket. I stupidly thought that by concealing my self-perceived flaws with a bright canary yellow jacket, my flaws would magically disappear and nobody would see them. In actual fact (and this is obvious to most normal people), adorning a bright yellow jacket has the entirely opposite effect to going unseen. For several stark reasons, one actually stands out more in this way because it just *aint* fashionable to wear the bright yellow uniform of an unpopular residence everywhere you go. *It was ridiculous.* For one, I was committing a fashion crime. *Who wears a bright canary yellow jacket made from quantec out of choice?* Whether it's to the library or to a social event, there is really no need to wear one's residence jacket outside the confines of the residence itself. None of the other res-mates ever wore theirs, they detested them as if they were infected. Besides, the jacket was only mandatory for first years anyway so me wearing it out and about certainly screamed that I was attempting to cover up, zip myself in, trap myself inside and keep others at a distance. I rarely left my room without it just in case I needed to cover up. I was like a child dragging their *blanky* along with them.

There was no roommate to urge me into the day or keep me in check so I withdrew into my dark single bedroom like a depressive recluse. It was in the dinginess of my room that I wallowed in self-pity and dissatisfaction, dreaming about a way of life I could have grabbed onto if I still had the resources within myself. But I didn't. It was just too much of an internal struggle to trigger the switch from the lazy absent me to the go-getter I always wanted to be and thought I would be and used to be once upon a time. I honestly could have stayed inside my room for days without letting in any sunlight and no one would have known because I had also disassociated myself from my first-year group of friends. The happy bunch with whom I used to have great adventures with. What a stupid thing to do, especially because my actions were purposeful! I wanted to pave my own way in my second year by proving I could do it all on my own, and look where it got me, lonely and unsatisfied. Writing this actually stirs up anger with 'the self' I once was because my actions were so blatantly self-sabotaging. *How could I have been so blind to my needs? How could I have let pride get the better of me like that? I was being stubborn, against myself. How ridiculous! I had the ability within me to make changes, why didn't I utilise them?*

I knew I had it in me to reach my goals. I knew I had it in me to get back on track, so why wasn't I allowing myself to do so. At the young age of seven-years-old, I opted to attend rather than miss a day of school when my family went away on holiday for a long weekend. I chose to miss out on the fun of a weekend away because I had already set out to achieve a school award for Seven Years Unbroken School Attendance that I could only potentially receive seven years later. And I did it. I won that award. The only one in my whole grade that year out of at least ninety students. That was me, those were the characteristics inside of me. *Where were they now? I was angry with myself. I was letting myself down on purpose. Why?*

I also remember withdrawing from the offer to serve on the house committee alongside all of my first-year friends because I didn't deem myself worthy of the position. I also conjured the ridiculous notion that it would be better for my development as an individual if I worked my way up the ranks instead of jumping straight to a position as an esteemed *Haka* member, (house committee) so I declined my nomination and opted for the lesser role of serving as a *voog* (mentor). *Stupid move pulling myself down when I was rightfully entitled to accept it!* I did the same silly thing in primary school when I voted for another girl instead of myself as Head Girl (head prefect) because I was afraid someone would find out that I voted for myself. In hindsight, voting for oneself says to the authorities you are willing to step up to the responsibility of serving others. I had worked hard for seven years to achieve that goal of being head prefect. I never missed one day of school, had great marks, had top cultural positions, was involved in the annual school drama plays, played in team sports, achieved in so many areas, and was happy and well-balanced. I simply loved primary school – those were fantastic years and all I wanted to do was serve my school well during my last year, but alas, it never happened in the way I had planned. I became prefect but not head prefect. I got over that disappoint soon afterwards, but it still stung for a while. *Life is full of curveballs that prepare you for the big journey.*

Snag #4: rock bottom results

After about the eighth week of that first semester in my second year of university, I was attending so few of my lectures that I barely had any study material from which to work with. I had missed the dates for all the tests and scopes for the examinations, so I was pretty much in the dark about most things. Due to this ridiculous lack of care and as a result of my non effort, I failed three semester subjects. To say I was mortified is an understatement. I hadn't really failed anything up until this point, let alone sixty percent of my semester subject's half-way through my second year. I was in a state of shock. The only positive that emerged from this mess is that I received a serious wake up call. I made a huge turn around in the second semester and ensured that I passed everything, and I did.

Unfortunately, my three failed subjects still lingered and my pride couldn't take it. There was no way I could possibly face anyone in my own year knowing that I had failed three subjects, or even worse witness me repeating them. They would all know. Or so I ridiculously assumed. Funnily though, I probably knew at the most three other student's names in a class of two-hundred-and-fifty large, so basically no one would have ever found out. I don't even think anyone would have even noticed or even cared. I was deathly embarrassed and couldn't bear the gossip (if any) and scandal (oh please!) about my failure. I could not risk them see me redoing the same subjects the following year. With this deep disgrace, I made a hasty and irrational decision - I was going to leave.

Snag #5: emotionally charged decision

In hindsight, it is a pity there was no one at university to guide me through this failure and decision-making process because their guidance and support would have reassured me immensely. At this point I thought my entire life was ruined by this academic failure of mine. *Because I had failed three subjects, my life just had to be over. There was no way I could regenerate from this.* This is how juvenile my thinking was. Obviously, I was only seeing the dilemma from my limited perspective and where I thought it bigger than it was, it really wasn't. *There is no way that failing three subjects in one semester at the age of nineteen would derail the rest of one's future or life. What a joke! How naïve!*

My assumption during this time was that I was the first person to have ever failed a subject at university – EVER! Later I found out that many students face obstacles while at university and need to redo subjects, some of whom also considered moving on to other pathways but rather stayed and then later received their qualification. Some students even had to redo semesters or entire years because in that year the subjects were only year subjects. Some students faced the death of loved ones just before their exam periods but still managed to pull through. The problem was, and this is a big problem (for many others as well), nobody knew the problem I was facing. The reason for me was: I hadn't admitted any of it because I was too proud – once again, so no one knew, so how *could* they have helped? And if you don't share your feelings or concerns with others, how will anyone be able to assist you. People can't sniff what's happening inside your brain or weighing on your heart, you must talk about it. Pride really stopped me from speaking up and moving forward. Pride muzzled my voice.

Now I am not looking for an escape goat to take the blame but one thing that did sadden me was that not one call was received from either the house mistress or the law faculty to query the reason for my sudden departure. I wonder if someone had followed up with me saying that it was going to be okay and that failing was not the end of the world and that nobody else actually cared or even really noticed, I would possibly not have left. On the other side though, would I have listened? I don't think so, because my prideful embarrassment had already consumed me. I felt hopelessly scared and needed a way out of the shameful mess I had found myself in. I had let so many people down, especially my parents. Considering that I wasn't achieving in any other area of life I felt it easier to just slip away unnoticed, under the radar (just as I had done in high school).

Clearly, I'm aware that universities have thousands of students registered at any given time, and cannot keep track of every student's progress because at a tertiary level people are expected to function on their own. So, for this reason I can understand why they didn't contact me. But if an academically sound student suddenly fails three subjects in one semester, there must be a reason for it. This area of student support should perhaps be addressed because there are those out there (including me) who didn't think they were worthy of counselling or support because either they feel they are solely responsible for their predicament or they just don't know that advice is a possibility. *Would I have listened though?*

Before entertaining the decision to leave, I came across a first-year student who had transferred from a correspondence university. She told me all about an institution where you don't have to attend classes and can work in your own time. *Wow! A way out of my predicament I thought.* This became my plan of action. I would return home and study full time where no one else would find out about my failure. A minor detail I chose to overlook when entertaining this idea of self-study, was that one needed self-discipline and time management skills to progress with studies at a correspondence university. Skills I clearly did not possess at this stage.

> **"Then Saul said to Samuel, "I have sinned, for I have transgressed the commandment of the Lord and your words, because I feared the people and obeyed their voice."**
> **- 1 Samuel 15:246**

Snag #6: removing the focus

After arriving back at home in 2004, I registered with the long-distance correspondence university she had spoken of to attempt continuing with my law degree. I was now 'at home' again but this time as a confirmed disappointment. With running from one university and carrying the stigma of three failed subjects, nothing was helping my crumbling self-esteem. As poor as I was in direction, I carried this diminishing self-confidence with me right into my now third year of legal studies and into my exams. Needless to say, I failed three more subjects. Only this time, it was not the scorn of my peers but the disdain of my parents that deepened the wound. A wound that was growing with every passing failure because it was becoming infected from so many sides.

I was now officially somebody I did not know.

High school was bad enough, but this was even worse because I thought I would have turned it all around by now. I hated myself, and this hatred led me through the second semester of that third year where I feared failing more modules so I only registered for two. I can't remember exactly if I passed these two but what I do have an exact memory of is the erratic nature of my bumpy movement through these studies at this correspondence university. The registering of and then cancelling of subjects halfway through the semester, the avoidance of completing assignments and the failure to submit them, the half-attempt at studying for exams and the stay away from examinations just grew into a monstrous cycle. Right through my law studies at this correspondence university, I never completed one non-obligation assignment (the large assignment vital in preparing for the examination). Anyone who understands how to succeed at studying at this university knows that these assignments are crucial. The state of my studies during these three years at home, after leaving that university in Johannesburg, was appalling.

One glimmer of hope during these three years came in the form of my mom compelling me to find some sort of work. So, in June of that first year back at home, I signed up at a local attorney's firm and joined the conveyancing department. Working gave me a morsel of purpose. It was also good to earn a bit of money and be part of a team headed by a dynamic woman who inspired us all to work hard for our department. She would reward us with monthly financial incentives which encouraged me even more. It was during this time that I bought 'the scooter' and later 'the Chevy Spark.' Two real achievements for me.

Overlapping with the sense of fulfilment I received from working, I also got for myself a real-life boyfriend (one that I didn't have to invent). I slimmed down tremendously and soon regained a whole load of self-esteem. The novelty of having a boyfriend and the success at work saw my studies taking a back seat though. I passed one subject here and one subject there, failing two here and three there, never completing any semester fully. A pattern that continued for the remainder of the three years while living in Kempton Park. *I was so desperately trying to figure things out and where I was meant to be.*

Eventually I became so embarrassed with my continuous rebellious choices that I tried keeping them from my family and friends. It was all one big juggling performance. I knew I wasn't doing right by my parents and honouring their wishes but I continued my personal sabotage anyway. *What an inside mess I was!* My parents felt that there was no longevity with the social situation I was in, but I continued at it anyway. *Deep down I knew it as well. I knew the choices I was making were because I wanted independence and to experience what others had always had so easily. I was torn. What was I searching for? What was I really aiming for? Who was I searching for?*

Combined with the shame of hardly making any academic progress during those three years, (2004–2007) with resenting the way I had let my parents down, I was now developing claustrophobic feelings in the social situation even I saw no future in. Inevitably, the wheels under my feet started spinning again. A life I had essentially never chosen for myself was slowly extinguishing my air supply and I began suffocating. The life I had not planned for was creeping in gradually before my eyes and if I didn't do something about it, it'd be too late to turn it around.

I had lost all sense of control.

Besides the deep shame I felt for dishonouring my parents' wishes and the overall pathetic academic progress I had barely made during the five years after finishing high school, the nut finally cracked one day. There I was standing in the detergent's aisle at the local supermarket scanning through household cleaners and dishwashing liquids when I started panicking. Having never experienced a panic attack before, I stood in shock as I gasped for air that wasn't coming. The thickening claustrophobic awareness of my chosen reality started choking me and all of a sudden, I couldn't breathe.

What was I doing?

I couldn't do this anymore. Who was I kidding? Who was I trying to fool? Of all the people I could fool, it shouldn't be me. How pointless would it be trying to fool myself, because not even I was happy with the way things were? Only I would be left bitter and regretful, not anyone else. I was the one who had to end up living with the choices I was making, nobody else. At the end of it, I was the one who would suffer more than anyone else for sticking with bad decisions that even I knew were wrong for me.

There was absolutely no way I was ready to be buying household cleaner, and definitely not at the immature age of twenty-two. I had to face reality. One bad choice after the next had led me to where I was that day standing in the supermarket with a cleaning product in one hand and my car keys in the other. The one would lead me down a path of regret and the other would lead me to a fresh start. So, I left the detergents right there in the aisle and made a decision. I was going to leave … again.

**Growth demands so much from you,
but it's the most worthwhile experience you will endure.**

Snag #7: the definition of stupid (hitting your head repeatedly thinking you'll get a different result every time)

At the end of 2007, I resigned from the attorney's firm and signed up for residence in a student commune in Hatfield, Pretoria (a forty-minute drive from Kempton Park). By moving there, I reckoned that the several nearby on-campus universities in Pretoria, as well as all the other students living in and around Hatfield would somehow magically release the secret formula of finding direction and purpose. I also thought that living in amongst students once again would motivate me to complete my studies and give me a sense of shared identity.

As long as I could remember, I had always wanted to stay in a commune and experience full student life so I moved into a house with three other housemates hoping that this would finally provide me with direction. This situation too was not conducive for studying and even though I met many kinds of people and worked in various jobs, midway through the year I discovered that I was even more confused than ever before. During that year I worked as a bar lady at an upmarket fashion café, a promotions consultant, a DJ, a video store clerk and an English test marker for a local private school. Working in these jobs was very exciting and at the same time beneficial, because I was able to dust off my need for curiosity. But still something was missing.

Salad days is a Shakespearean idiomatic expression meaning *a youthful time, accompanied by the inexperience, enthusiasm, idealism, innocence, or indiscretion that one associates with a young person.*

It was in the commune that I tried my first cigarette. Being an adamant non-smoker for the preceding twenty-two years of my life, I emphasised to the other girls that I would never buy my own packet of cigarettes. This I thought would prevent me from getting addicted and becoming an official smoker. Needless to say, by week three I was buying my own packs. The routine action of lighting a smoke became a stabling factor for me and helped relieved much of the pressure during this time. I really enjoyed this social systematic activity and will actually always look back at this smoking phase in my twenties with a strange fondness. I shall call these *my salad days*.

In June of the year living in Hatfield, I decided to return to my first university, because I wasn't coping with this self-study portion but still had to see out the remaining six months of the rental agreement in the commune through. My decision was to attempt full time university once again in one final effort to finish my legal studies. This too proved to be futile because by June of the following year, 2008, I had only passed two subjects. It had finally been confirmed, I just wasn't interested in pursuing this degree or this direction of study. When I learned that I owed the initial university outstanding fees, I started working as a legal secretary at a law firm in Rosebank to pay back my debt. So, with the salary I earned, I paid rent, tried to pay car instalments, bought groceries, and petrol. Thankfully my medical aid was still being paid for by my Dad.

During the two years after leaving the commune in Hatfield, I stayed in various cities. Edenvale, Bryanston, and Centurion. I moved back to Kempton Park and then lived at three different places in the city of Kempton Park alone. During this tumultuous time, I had slept in my car, carted furniture and my belongings back and forth between all these places using the tiniest boot and back seat as packing space, almost had my car repossessed for non-payment, worked as an au-pair for two separate families, drove hundreds and hundreds of kilometres around Gauteng, got caught up in the rat race and played live *Texas Holdem* at night to earn extra cash. I was so lost and searching for answers. *Where was I meant to be? What was I meant to be doing?*

After I left the Rosebank law firm in 2010, I started working as a Personal Assistant at a company close to central Johannesburg, but this job only lasted for roughly six months as a result of retrenchment. I then started at a very glamorous property company in Sandton which also only lasted two months. During the years of 2002 and 2011, I worked in everything from photography to office administration, from recruitment to disc jockeying, from secretarial work to legal work, from promotions to marking test papers, from bar work to waitressing, from au pairing to more office work, I tried it all. Using every bit of it to figure out who I was and where I was meant to be as I still had no idea. During these years I sat through many interviews, so many in fact that I was no longer nervous for them. I knew I belonged somewhere, I just didn't know how to get there. Finding the right work was important to me and crucial to my sense of belonging because it meant fulfilment and a sense of purpose.

Snag #8: ignoring my unique talents and gifts was the same as denying who I was created to be

I had been given talents and gifts that were unique to me but during those years I had been denying them. I was artistic and creative but thought it beneath me to study art or anything in this direction because art was not seen as 'clever enough' or 'well-paid enough' or 'esteemed enough' as Law was.

The Parable of the Talents

"For the kingdom of heaven is like a man traveling to a far country, who called his own servants and delivered his goods to them. And to one he gave five talents, to another two, and to another one, to each according to his own ability; and immediately he went on a journey. Then he who had received the five talents went and traded

with them, and made another five talents. And likewise he who had received two gained two more also. But he who had received one went and dug in the ground, and hid his lord's money. After a long time the lord of those servants came and settled accounts with them.

So he who had received five talents came and brought five other talents, saying, 'Lord, you delivered to me five talents; look, I have gained five more talents besides them.' His lord said to him, 'Well done, good and faithful servant; you were faithful over a few things, I will make you ruler over many things. Enter into the joy of your lord.' He also who had received two talents came and said, 'Lord, you delivered to me two talents; look, I have gained two more talents besides them.' His lord said to him, 'Well done, good and faithful servant; you have been faithful over a few things, I will make you ruler over many things. Enter into the joy of your lord."
- Matthew 14:12-30

THAT DREADUL SUNDAY MORNING

It was one Sunday morning that changed it all for me. The events that followed would set into motion the catalyst I desperately needed to see things clearly and face up to the truth about my choices and where they would ultimately lead me.

My life was about to change drastically.

THE WORST KIND OF PHONE CALL

This particular morning, I had parked at a shopping centre in Kempton Park, one I knew very well. I had watched it expand over the years from a field of grass to a bustling complex of upmarket shops and restaurants and now I found myself just waiting in the parking lot. Just waiting, for no real reason. I really had nothing to do there, nothing I couldn't buy in the city I did live in and had just driven from. Perhaps it was the familiarity of the surroundings that continuously urged me to drive back there time and time again. In effect, I had just driven fifty kilometres to sit in my car and wait. Wait for something, I don't know, just wait. This is how I spent my time these days anyway, wondering from city to city for answers.

It was around eleven o'clock and after already having driven aimlessly around Kempton Park, I finally decided to park and remain in my car. For at least twenty minutes I just sat there, staring at the steering wheel while puffing on a cigarette. As per usual I was directionless, without any plan or purpose for the day, but strangely there was something different about this morning. Even though I was following my regular pattern of driving pointlessly around the city's streets, I felt as if there was something *hanging in the air*.

And then it happened, my phone rang. It was my aunt. In a clear and urgent voice, she said.

"Hi Candy. Pat has been killed in a car accident."

?

?

?

?

What!

Wait!

What!

Wait a minute.

My cousin Pat.

No way.

I don't believe it.

There's no way.

He can't be dead.

There is no way.

What!?

The call ended.

This is what the lagging-of-time had been the whole morning. This is what had taken place. This is what it was.

Oh no! This is terrible! This is the worst news of all.

Immediately I called my aunt and said, "I'm coming over."

THIS CAN'T BE REAL

Nothing prepares you for a moment like this, the moment when you receive a call about sudden death. The rawness of those words. They're so numbing, so stabbing. At first your heart pounds through your chest and then your body goes limp. You don't know whether to cry or to scream or run into the street yelling. Initially you can't accept the news because the gravity of it is too overwhelming to comprehend. Wild thoughts rush through your brain like maybe that person isn't even dead, maybe they're sleeping and can be woken up or perhaps they're only injured. I even imagined that I would be able to wake him up, if only I could just get there quick enough. One grasps for any form of reassurance when the reality is too difficult to digest.

GRASPING FOR PERSPECTIVE

Any funeral is sad, but when the loss touches you extremely personally, somehow, you're given a small window through which to look out into your own life. With this slight view of reality shifting, you're able to take a look at how you are living the only life you have been given. In a way, death serves the living because it provides one with critical perspective. In the days and months following a personal death, one is forced backwards and forwards in time because you're confronted with the hard realisation of your own frailty and how far it really stretches.

Pat was only thirty-one years old. He had a young wife and three small children. He had been raised wonderfully and was such an asset to the world. Words couldn't even describe how heart-breaking this was for me.

Where does one go from here?

What does one do with this level of impact?

How does one translate such a personal tragedy into something coherent? The sheer tragedy of it. It was too colossal.

I even wondered why it wasn't me instead. He had a family and I was a lost mess wasting my time. During that week after his death, 'my entire world' shifted. This was a serious wake up call. This was it; it was now or never.

The life I had always dreamed of living was slipping through my fingers and soon I would find myself in the very regretful position of not being able to turn back to it.

It was time for change.

Drastic change.

GAINING PERSPECTIVE

With all the struggle and despair I'd been experiencing, it was my cousin's death that catapulted everything into perspective for me almost immediately. For me personally, *this tragedy was not in vain* because it gave me the hard knock I had been desperately craving. The young life that Pat had, just snatched away so suddenly one Sunday morning after church shot right to my heart. I couldn't ignore the awakening pain.

It was time to react. It was time for a life changing decision.

In the weeks that followed, after years of wrestling and tugging to and fro. I finally decided to end the destructive affair I was having with Law.

To my parents' dismay, I officially ended my legal studies completely. I was done. *Who was I kidding?* I couldn't possibly continue beating the dead horse of 'this failed course of life' any longer. I was tired of job hopping and not knowing where to work. I was tired of not knowing where I belonged. I was tired of not knowing where to live. I was tired of failing subjects and struggling to achieve what was clearly not intended for me. I had finally decided that enough was enough and now was the time to call the end to my decade long struggle. My plan: start fresh.

A NEW CHAPTER ON A CLEAN PAGE

For six years since the end of high school, well actually even before that, I battled with identifying with the person who had hijacked my body and was using me to live out their aimless state of confusion. Whoever it was, it wasn't me. All these years I had been denying my God-given talents and purpose and it was time to accept this as part of the reason why I was feeling so out-of-place. I was not doing what I was designed to do. I was not living purpose filled. I would have wasted my life and denied myself a chance of becoming who I was uniquely set out to be if I didn't acknowledge my distinct abilities, interests and purpose.

I remember thinking at the time around my cousin's passing that if I had died at the young age that he did, which would have been four years from then, what would I have fulfilled? I would have lived in emptiness and died with a regret because I had spent my time being a version of someone else. Even at that stage, with my very underdeveloped comprehension of the truth of God's word, I knew that each one of us had been designed as originals and not copies of another and so we should not live as such. Even the physical uniqueness of our fingerprints demonstrate that we touch the world around us in a way that another cannot.

So why had I battled to end the struggle for so many years before if I already knew all of this?

... because I still had one major problem.

A weakness I couldn't let go of. It had crept its way into the decision-making process of ending my legal studies for all those years

... pride.

My pride wouldn't allow it.

All this time I had still been too proud to let go of the status that surrounded Law. I was too proud to let go of the compliments that came my way, "She's going to be a lawyer you know," or "Don't mess with her she's an attorney." A lot of attention and glory came my way because of my association with the legal fraternity and I didn't want to lose it. Even though this glory made me feel important, deep down I knew it was false because I was struggling so much. I had grabbed onto this momentary high of arrogance that those who know and wield the law possess and I didn't want to let go for fear of losing my *puffed-up* impression to the world. This is why I held on for so long. This is why I held on so tightly. It was my temporary man-made identity.

So, what then changed? What led me to make that final decision to end it all?

I finally decided to put pride aside, and give 'being truly honest with myself' a go.

DEATH IN PRIDE

It was my cousin's death that triggered me to realise that pride wasn't going to get me anywhere. Pride was leading me nowhere. I simply couldn't hold onto it if I wanted to move on and live my life. It was keeping me back, and for what, for false praise? I had to stop caring what others thought and imagined. I had to stop putting so much stock into other people's opinion. I just simply couldn't hold onto it any longer. I had to let it go.

... *'it had taken a death to breathe new life into me.'*

My dear cousin impacted my life in a way he would never know. His death touched me so deeply that it helped save me.

**Even so we, when we were children, were in bondage
under the elements of the world. - Galatians 4:3**

Once I had let go of my pride, I could move on to being honest with myself. So much of my pride was because I was worried what others would think and say about my actions. But really when it came down to it, and this you only realise in hindsight, is that nobody else really cares as much as you think they do. Nobody else, especially friends and colleagues, were lying awake at night considering why I had made the decisions I did. Nobody else was driving to work steam rolling through ideas as to why I had stopped studying Law. Maybe they gave my decision a thought, but really my choices were my own and didn't affect others as much as I thought they did. So why all the worrying about what others might think? One big reason was because of the pride I had in my *intellect and abilities*. I simply couldn't let go of the status that I was 'smart' and studying Law complimented this so perfectly. The esteem that came with becoming a lawyer was too alluring to hold on to. It was too seductive. But this appeal was false and I would have surely died if I had held onto it.

**... but of the tree of the knowledge of good and
evil you shall not eat, for in the day that you eat
of it you shall surely die. - Genesis 2:17**

CHOOSING THE TRUTH

The moment I finally made the decision to end my legal studies completely, I felt such immense relief. The only hurdle left was informing my parents. They had worked so hard to support me at every level, so naturally it was disappointing to let them down. But I had no choice. I had to do this.

Even though I was ending my legal studies, I was not ending my education. I still wanted to obtain a degree. My plan going forward was to change from Law to a degree where I could utilise more of my natural interests and talents. God had given me special gifts of creativity and denying them any longer would have sucked the life from me.

When the time came to choose my new career path and start studying again, I sat at my desk and said out loud, "What would I choose to study if no one else was in the picture, just me? What would I study if no one else had to know?" For me to reach this answer, I had to leave everyone else's opinion out of the equation in order to be truthful and honest. This decision couldn't be influenced by anyone else. This time, it had to be me and God. God had already shown me that I was unique, which meant that I had been given unique talents and gifts and desires.

What would I pick, regardless of how 'unintellectual' or 'unacclaimed' it seemed to be to the world? What would I pick without pride affecting my decision? And there it was, with a humble heart I saw it. A Bachelor of Arts in Languages and Literature with specialisation in Creative Writing. *What! A Bachelor of Arts – wow - what a 360!*

Once I had registered at the same correspondence university I had suffered through previously, but this time from a place of humility, I dove right in. It wasn't long before I was half way through my course and achieving excellent marks. *This was definitely the course for me.* In fact, I did so well that in the end I was offered to apply for a fully paid honours bursary to further my studies. I simply loved the subject material because it was well suited to my interests and talents. Serendipitously, it is this branch of knowledge in the faculty of Human Sciences where I happened to stumble onto the eye-opening subject of Linguistics. Through the science of language (study of Linguistics), the Lord stirred something palpable in me that would transform me indefinitely. Through His branch of the knowledge of language, my eyes were opened.

By humility *and* the fear of the LORD
***Are* riches and honor and life. - Proverbs 22:4**

CANDACE ANNE

Second area pride affected: relationships

"Children, obey your parents in the Lord, for this is right. Honour your father and mother, which is the first commandment with a promise: that it may be well with you and you may live long on the earth. And you, fathers, do not provoke your children to wrath, but bring them up in the training and admonition of the Lord." - Ephesians 6:1-4

Not long after I went back home after my two-year stint at the first university with my tail between my legs, I started dating a guy who I would date for the next three to five years. During this time though, I rebelled against my parents' wishes and truthfully even against myself. I knew deep down that it was all only temporary but the relationship was timely and crucial to helping me grow in so many ways, so I really needed the exposure.

With this relationship, I landed into a social mix that opened my eyes to another side of life I had never seen before. This part of it was very good for me. Most of the people were of a foreign nationality and lived and survived without their immediate families who still lived in their home country. The younger generation's move to South Africa was a chance at economic success and most of them found it because of their savvy and entrepreneurial know-how. Spending time with this crowd allowed me to see life from another perspective. Never before had I witnessed so much from another part of the world without actually leaving my own country. I got first-hand experience with another culture, heritage and language. What a fascinating learning curve for me.

There was a flip side though to this window of exploration. Not only did I experience the exciting part of it but also caught a glimpse at another side of life. Coming from the particular family household I had, it was clear to see the contrast in the way I had been raised. There was a clear difference in values, beliefs, backgrounds and attitudes. I saw how teenage children grew up overnight when distanced from their parents and how they had to rely on their own resources to thrive. I also saw how financial backing impacted options in ways I had never before witnessed. My Dad has always maintained, "What you see, depends on where you sit." A sentiment I was able to see play out first hand. You will undoubtedly only be able to give an account of something you have personally witnessed. But this account is also affected by where you see the scene from. Our locations and experiences impact our version of events. Everyone then has a differing perspective because of where they are situated.

The few years I spent with this crowd was like taking a travel gap year in a foreign country or doing an overseas exchange program without ever even using my passport. These people had been schooled by another kind of school, a school where life lessons were not learnt from textbooks but from being resourceful. Their weeks were broken up into segments of income producing opportunities, allowing for flexibility when a business opportunity arose. Also known as: the streetwise. Most importantly though, even though they were all streetwise and resourceful, they all still had common sense.

Despite their lifestyles, drugs never entered the scene and was never even spoken of but if it had, I would have left immediately. We all possessed a basic common sense and even though I was still *searching* and *going through a phase*, none of us were fools. At the core I knew what I accepted and what I didn't. I remember learning in primary school that, "If you don't start, you can't get hooked." My Mom's own words passed down from my Grandfather also remained with me, "Never let anything control you." These small teachings were priceless.

Common sense surpasses education.
It is not the same in reverse.

Their spontaneous day to day approach to living was very exciting for a while, but in the long term it was not sustainable and my parents always knew this (deep down so did l). At some point or another, one must seek to plant somewhere or take root, or else your life becomes a series of episodes that gets swept up wherever the wind takes you. Because my parents continually insisted on me cutting ties, I hung on longer than I should of even though I knew I didn't fit in completely. The more they pushed against it, the more I resisted. Pride kept me clinging on, pride kept me from admitting I was holding on to spite them. The pride I had in making my own choices, "I know what I am doing, I don't need any help from anybody, I can do this all by myself," really did keep me lingering longer than I should of. *Really senseless I'd say especially when my actions were self-sabotaging! I don't know why it's human nature to do this, it's just in us to push harder against what we know is right for us. I know of other people who also protest in resistance against the good authority in their lives. Why do we do it? Why do we actively do the opposite of what we've been told.* The last thing I wanted to do was admit to my parents that they were right and that I had been mistaken. I wanted all of it to be my decision and especially not because *they had told me so.* It was the classic case of late adolescent-young adult rebellion where I was struggling to formulate my own identity and establish a dimension of independent decision-making. As adolescents do, I was trying to figure things out on my own and who I really was. I wanted my choices and the results of these choices to be mine. I was trying to figure out where I belonged.

For a long while my pride blocked any consideration to how my parents felt because I was too stubborn to see their point. I didn't want to be seen as not being smart enough to make wise choices, *I know what I am doing and who are you to tell me otherwise,* so I never really heard their plight.

In some unique instances, one must be allowed the freedom, time and space to test what one expects from life. When I say 'test', I am referring to the careful and thoughtful comparison one makes when assessing the differences between what they know to be right and what others might say. One must be able to venture safely through unknown territory yet have the co-ordinates to return to their rightful place. One must be allowed to place what they have been taught, mostly values and beliefs, alongside another set of values and determine for themselves if what they believe to be true, is really true? In a way, a kind of grace period. This is what I was doing. I was unknowingly testing the way I had been trained up in against an alternative set of values and principles. Essentially, I was weighing up my teachings against other life theories and choices. Very soon it would become evident which column emerged as stronger and more convincing.

Train up a child in the way he should go,
And when he is old he will not depart from it. - Proverbs 22:6

A parent can train their child up in the correct way, in the Lord's way, but in the end, it is ultimately the individual's decision as to which way they will go. For this reason, parents must continually cover their children in prayer. Praying ceaselessly. Thankfully my parents trained me well as a child as well. They took me to Sunday School, showed me how to read the Bible and pray, and lived out and applied the importance of strong family values. It was this right foundation that had me rooted but my branches were the ones flapping about in the wind. It was this foundation that I held onto during my darkest moments of despair and wandering. It was this foundation that drew me back to my rightful place. It was this right foundation that saved me. As a child, I was taught by my Mom to correctly fear the Lord, to fear Judgment Day and eternal punishment. I was taught that one day we would all answer to the Lord and give account of our lives. It was this teaching that continued flaming ever so dimly in the far reaches of my mind all throughout my wandering, and that made me aware of the path of error I was walking. I knew that I needed to return to the Lord's way one day and that this wandering was momentary.

Hire a teenager while they still know everything.

Regrettably, the longer and harder my parents persisted, the longer I resisted their requests. This resistance caused tension which only led to frustration and conflict. Pride had slithered its way into the middle of everything and was not only affecting my current relationships but possibly also my future ones. Because I was not letting go of the situation I was in, I was in effect taking precious time from building relationships in which I would find a shared identity. Perhaps even from the one I was intended to marry. This is the same as not letting go of one's past and so allowing it to affect your future by not moving on or letting go.

In practical terms, instead of being unattached and available to receive the interests of 'my potential husband', I was out on Saturdays and Sundays watching sport and sitting through hours and hours of online poker. I would hang around aimlessly or sleep in the car while everyone else watched computer games and played FIFA – activities I found mundanely boring. So instead of being in an environment that would facilitate me moving on, I was floating in between two worlds, each pulling me in separate directions. Until I decided for *myself* that this was not what I wanted, nothing would have changed. I had to be downright honest with myself. Be truthful, be real. This was when I decided to leave Kempton Park and head for Hatfield, Pretoria and move into the commune.

Throughout these years of searching and resisting, I held onto the fifth commandment of the Ten Commandments written down by Moses for God's people. It lingered continually.

Honor your father and your mother, that your days may be long upon the land which the LORD your God is giving you. - Exodus 20:12

I felt that not surrendering to my parents' requests, I was possibly causing myself long-term harm because the commandment that I was not observing came with a promise. The promise that "your days may be long upon the land which the LORD your God is giving you", was being ignored and this concerned me. I did not want to not receive this promise because of my prideful rebellion, so I began evaluating the situation from another perspective - God's perspective. The problem with humans in general is that we spend so much time considering how we feel about God, and not much time on how God feels about us.

Even though Ephesians 6:1-2 can be a touchy section of scripture within Christian families because there is dispute around the extent of how far obedience reaches, and what part of life does honour refer to, and until what age does it reach, and at what point do you leave your parents' authority, and does authority only apply to parents who are right with the Lord. In the end, it is the heart of scripture that matters. What is God saying to us? What is at the heart of the Scripture: love. He is not saying to us, interpret it according to your own situation by taking your circumstances and feelings into consideration, He is saying what He is saying because He knows what is good and right for you, so obey it. He is saying to trust Him because He knows what is best.

Because the verse in Ephesians resonates with me personally, I will take the intention of the verse from where it comes. The place of origin being God's heart. *What was God's intention with the commandment? Was it to keep a beloved child safe or to harm them?* Originally part of the Ten Commandments in the Old Testament, but also found in the New Testament, I feel it is our duty as children of God to honour our fathers and mothers because just as I was given unto my parents as a gift, they were given to me as a gift from God Himself and these are blessings we must treasure. I didn't have to look too far for reasons as to how my parents were a blessing to me because I simply compared them to what I was witnessing around me. It became clear to me that my parents had put in one hundred percent effort with raising their children.

I had a father and mother who adored me and who loved me from the moment I was thought of. They strived to raise me in the right way and wanted the best for me. They considered my future thoughtfully and with great care and wanted to educate me so I would have the right opportunities available. They wanted me to find the right man, a God-fearing man with whom I could raise children with. Until this point in my life, I was not honouring them at all and so felt that I was violating something even greater than their mortal longing for me to find my way. I was not honouring my position as a child of God and so denying my own blessings. All along, throughout this trying time, my parents obviously only wanted the best for me. Something a child only learns after the fact. If this means risking being the bad guy as a parent by enduring rejection just so that I could see the situation from their angle, they faced up to it. Their willingness to face rebuke showed me just how much they really cared for me.

Still to this day, I am thankful that my parents fought for me, as I couldn't imagine my life turning out any other way.

I am also thankful for their grace during this tumultuous time and for the love they demonstrated when I returned. *Thank you so much, Mom and Dad.*

FINALLY, ... CAME THE REQUEST I COULDN'T IGNORE

For years my parents begged and encouraged, reasoned and demanded that I complete my legal studies through which I suffered in darkness and despair, alone and hopeless.

For years my parents nagged and pleaded, groaned and probed for me to move on to a more promising relationship.

For years I endured the lying, misleading, hiding, dishonesty, frustration, confusion, isolation, struggle, heartache, pain, anxiety, depression, anguish, pleading, all with many tears. Until one day

... came the request I couldn't ignore.

A KNIGHT IN SHIINING ARMOUR

I wake up shivering. Carefully I lift my head to see where I am and realise I'm lying face down in a field of muddy grass with dirty rainclouds rumbling overhead. Even though I'm covered in mud and see the grumbling clouds threatening to burst open, my quivering body doesn't move. *Why am I here? How did I get here? Where am I?* Tears stream down my cheeks as I struggle to think of the answers. *Why don't I just get up? What is wrong with me?* My body shakes uncontrollably as I lie soaked in cold mud. *Why don't I do something? Why don't I just get up?*

I must get up. I must keep moving. Get up Candace, get up! Struggling to see through the wet hair clinging to my face, I stumble to my feet. A cold wind blows and beats the drenched clothes tightly against my trembling body. Battling to stand I try moving forward in any direction but lose balance and fall into the wet mud. Hopelessly, I start sobbing. *How did I get here? Why am I here? Did I come here myself? Where am I? Why would I be here?*

In the distance I notice a vague blurry figure approaching. I can't see much but sense myself drifting both to and from this field, as if I am really somewhere else and the field exists parallel to another place. *I am so confused, where am I?* As the figure draws nearer, the wind turns warmer and a stream of familiar memories float into my mind. They come and go but then slowly fade.

The figure is much nearer to me now. Suddenly a gust of cold wind shoots across the field between us and the rainclouds darken. Squinting my eyes, I see the figure more clearly as it approaches and it is a man on a horse. He trots to where I am lying drenched in mud, extends his arm for me to grab his hand and in one bold muscular swoop hoists me onto the horse with him. I almost fall as a vicious wind tries to whip me to the ground but he grabs me and places me firmly behind him.

The rider turns his head towards me and through the howling wind and darkening angry sky shouts, "I've got you, hold on!" With a flick of the reins, the horse jolts with a stallion's strength and we head off across the field.

Galloping away from the storm, a comforting security surrounds me. The wind warms up and calms the further we ride from the tempest. I know I am safe now; I am not sure how, I just know. Somehow, I trust this rider. We gallop for miles across the vast fields but say nothing to one another. Slowly I take my first deep breath and close my eyes to soak in the warm fresh breeze blowing through my hair. The only sound in this vastness is the rhythmic beating of the horse's hooves on the hard ground beneath us and its strong breathing. With not a cloud in sight now, all we see before us are the brush strokes of an orange and pink sky. It feels welcoming. My grip around the rider's waste loosens as we slow down to absorb the scenery and breathe in the sweet smell of the lush field around us. I breathe in … and he breathes in. The warm clean air fills our lungs. Finally, I am home.

Around the time I met this mysterious rider, I was still floating in a stormy state of confusion about where my life was heading. I really was standing on the brink of self-loathing. Even though I would never have done anything drastic, I had wondered to the edge of a very gloomy place because I felt dreadfully defeated in so many areas of my life. The stress of all this failure was naturally starting to weigh me down.

A lot was happening all at once. I was in the breakup phase of the relationship I had been in for ages, was moving from one place of accommodation to the next, had no clue which career path to pursue after abandoning my legal studies, and felt generally utterly hopelessly lost. All I could do was the only thing I knew to do, tug at my last ounce of optimism and positive attitude to get me through this mental and emotional torture of bewilderment. If I didn't take in air soon, I am not sure how long I could have gone on suffocating. I needed a break, and even though surprisingly I had an idea of what I wanted for my life, I just didn't know how to get there.

I was dying on the inside and the worst part was - nobody knew. Nobody had a clue of how desperate I was, how frustrated I was, and how agonising these years had been. It's one thing lying to everyone else but lying to yourself is the most harmful thing to do. The effect of this ongoing circle of lies is that your world becomes shallow because nothing has depth anymore. Every time I lied; the words scratched at my conscience. I knew they were wrong but I couldn't help myself because it got easier and more convincing every time I did it. I was only trying to make myself feel a little better and build myself up, especially when I compared my crumbling situation to others. I wonder now if my friends and family ever knew I was spinning a yarn of wool right before their eyes and were just too polite or bored to correct me and challenge the absurdity of what I sometimes conjured up. No one ever said anything to my face, but I am sure one or two must have walked away thinking, "Wow, what a load of croc, does she really expect me to believe all that?"

Not knowing where to live, where to work, where I was meant to be living, what work I was meant to be doing, who I was meant to be with, who I was meant to be striving towards becoming, was torturous.

I can still remember these awful feelings so clearly, even as I sit here typing word after word all these years later, the emotions trickle back. Reading through this, as I write, transports me to how horrendous those days and nights were. I would park at a shopping centre with no reason to be there other than to smoke cigarettes in my car and watch the other drivers climb in and out of their vehicles. I'd watch them walk into the store, climb back into their car and then head off to a place they knew they had to be. They had a plan, a destination to go, a place to be at, I didn't. I didn't know where I needed to be. Watching them gave me a sense of purpose though. *How stupid!* I would sit in my peach orange Chevy Spark just staring at them, contemplating whether I would come off as nutty if I sprinted from my car to ask them where they were heading. Maybe, just maybe,

For years my parents pressed, for years I hated my choices, for years I beat at a dead career, for years I dragged along a fading relationship, for years I hauled my pride with me … and then one day.

they would give me a clue as to where I was meant to be heading. Maybe they would let me follow them to a place of purpose, maybe they would introduce me to one of their family members who could then hand me an instruction manual of how to get where I needed to be. Ridiculous as this sounds, I actually thought that a random stranger could provide me with answers to my burning questions.

Fortunately, I suppose, the only thing I did have going for me was that I was motivated in finding a solution. I never once gave up. I never once quit at searching. The urge in overcoming is what saved me from quitting.

Never give up. Never ever give up.

THE MEETING

One sunny Friday morning, a butterfly flew in through my bedroom window. It flapped around for a while and then landed on my desk. The tiny creature lingered there for a moment, just long enough for its presence to mean something.

I chose to celebrate my twenty-fifth birthday with friends of mine at a paintball shooting range. The day was going according to plan until my friend and her boyfriend brought along a 'gate-crashing friend' of theirs to join in on the fun of paintball. This wasn't a problem because we were a big group and the more people to play, the better for everyone. After the paintballing session, we then all sat around *braaiing boerewors* (barbequing sausages) for lunch.

This was the day I saw the rider coming from afar.

The 'gate crasher' and I chatted comfortably and at length. It turned out that this 'gate crasher' liked me. During the weeks that followed, the four of us (my friend, her boyfriend and the 'gate crasher'), went out as a group of friends.

During those couple of weeks, the four of us had a great time hanging out until one freezing cold evening after a night out, my little peach orange machine froze. The car just wouldn't start. It was then that 'the gate crasher', whose name was Ryan, stepped up and offered to fix the problem. Once he had got the vehicle running, he cleverly gave me his number to call him if anything went wrong. *Smart move I'd say! The ball was now in my court to see whether I liked him back.*

Soon afterwards, after weeks of messaging and phone calls, Ryan asked me to be his date to a squash awards night; I was thrilled. At first, I was fearful about moving on because I had been so bewildered for so long but Ryan was a true gentleman and treated me like a princess, so I was greatly comforted. Fear about an unknown relationship and the unfamiliarity of it all was clinging on though. But, if I didn't let go of this fear, I would only rob myself.

For God has not given us a spirit of fear, but of power and of love and of a sound mind. – 2 Timothy 1:7

The night progressed very well, but when we got up to dance and he knew how to dance in the exact way I had been taught growing up, and very well too, I couldn't believe it. I was thrilled once again. I had always wanted to find a man who could *langarm* or *sokkie* (Afrikaans-South African style of dancing) because I enjoyed it very much. Here all this time I had only pictured myself with one person. I thought there was no hope, only fear, but there on the dance floor that night, it all changed for me. I suddenly felt extremely hopeful.

Several weeks passed and we saw a lot more of each other and that's when he asked me to be his girlfriend, and then asked again, and again, and then again. *What was getting in the way of me saying yes?* Even though I loved being around him because our connection was effortless, I kept saying no. He treated me so well and we were having so much fun, I just couldn't get my head around the feeling that this was it, this was the man that could possibly be my husband.

No ways! It couldn't be true! So soon, we had only just met. How did I feel like this? Shouldn't I be single for a while? Shouldn't I enjoy this new scene, you know, isn't that what they say I should do. It's my time now, they say. Even though deep down I felt the need and desire to settle down and find my husband, I should be single instead – shouldn't I? Even though I was dying inside and craving direction, guidance and security, I should get out there instead, isn't that what they say I should do. I should enjoy this feeling of singledom, shouldn't I? That's what 'they' say I must do. I'm aching inside because I feel that he could be the one for me but I can't give in so quickly, can I? I really adore this man but I've got this hardcore working girl exterior covering for me now and it masks my anguish so skilfully, I can't give that up. Let me just carry on with this pride some more, it might present me with a solution. Even though I still don't know where I am supposed to live, or work or what to do next, I am sure I can figure this out on my own soon enough.

And then one day

    … it started happening.

Even through this wrestling, I continued seeing Ryan because I really liked being around him, especially because he treated me like a princess and because we clicked so effortlessly. But, and a big but, I was still so jumbled. In hindsight I was shamefully misled. *Misled by who? Misled by what?*

I was so confused by it all. I knew that I wanted to be with Ryan but was so charmed by the idea of finally being that single chick in her twenties that I kept along with the charade of seeking the identity *they* were expecting me to go for. It was as if someone had been dangling a shiny object in front of me and I couldn't take my eyes off it. The immature me was chasing an image conjured by years of *Hollywood-glamour-mag moulding* because everyone who had achieved this look and lifestyle seemed to have achieved success and happiness (well from what was portrayed). To me, this glossy professional city slicker ideal looked so appealing and so I duplicated it. I wore the power suits (pencil skirts and fitted jackets), the high heels and the dark glasses. With a cigarette in one hand, my long straightened brunette hair and the car stereo pumping my favourites tunes. I had this conjured up version of myself that was blindly dragging me in conflicting directions. I felt so torn. From moving from one rental apartment to the next, to calling it quits on a career path I thought I'd have, to having no career path at all, to periodic job hopping, to hanging on to a previous fading relationship, I no longer had a shred of clarity on which way to turn. I was drowning, and still nobody knew.

Until one day

... I heard a voice.

"Go to Ryan"

Three words, "Go to Ryan," … that was it.

"Go to Ryan,"

"Go to Ryan,"

What! What? What was that?

Where was that coming from?

Who was that?

What!!!

This was the first time I had ever experienced anything like this. An audible voice with actual words I could understand. But from where?

Just three words, "Go to Ryan."

I could hear them clearly as if the person was standing right next to me and speaking directly into my ear.

Where were they coming from because there was no one standing next to me?

Strangely, even though I could hear the words, I wasn't only receiving them through my ears. They were also above me, around me, even through me. It was unreal – something I had never experienced before.

It was definite and affirming, loud yet intimate. It was totally new and unfamiliar to me, completely surreal. Words had surrounded me and filled me yet there was no one standing there to give them. Even if there was another person sitting right next to me at that moment, they wouldn't have heard a single one of the words being spoken, because the words weren't happening in the natural physical world.

Even though I had never heard something like this before, somehow, I knew what it was and even better, who it was. *How incredible!*

You don't know how you know; you just know. You can't describe it.

It's a knowing that surpasses all human understanding and explanation.

... and after the earthquake a fire, *but* the Lord *was* **not in the fire; and after the fire a still small voice. So it was, when Elijah heard *it*, that he wrapped his face in his mantle and went out and stood in the entrance of the cave. Suddenly a voice *came* to him, and said, "What are you doing here, Elijah?" - 1 Kings 19:13**

There's a mystery surrounding these experiences because they're so sacred. One can even doubt what happened because it all happens so quickly and intimately, but when you stop to think about what you experienced – you say to yourself, "Yeah that really did happen, that was real."

**... the mystery which has been hidden from
ages and from generations, but now has been
revealed to His Saints. - Colossians 1:26**

Being Heaven sent, the purity of the words are so averse to *the flesh* that they barely skim the surface of a mere mortal. I suppose this is why the words come as a whispering declaration and pass over ever so slightly – they cannot bare to linger – they are too Holy, and I am too blemished, too sinful.

Am **I a God near at hand," says the** Lord,
**"And not a God afar off?
Can anyone hide himself in secret places,
So I shall not see him?" says the** Lord;
**"Do I not fill heaven and earth? says
the** Lord. **- Jeremiah 23:23-24**

Why "Go" to Ryan, why not "Be with Ryan"? For a brief moment I pondered on my instructions, not to negate them but to try and grasp them even more. Perhaps the word "Go" was used because He was sending me away, getting me to move from my current stale position to the one alongside Ryan. Just like the word 'apostle' that means 'to be sent'.

Analysis aside, the words were pretty clear. I wasn't disputing them, just reflecting. How wonderful too that God had even called Ryan by name and had prepared him to receive me. Neither of us realised this at this stage though.

Why had God spoken to me? Why now? I certainly hadn't been walking in His will for the longest while. Funny thing though, despite being so confused throughout my dark decade of despair, I had always prayed continuously, wherever I was. In the car, in the bathroom, at work, while driving, in a waiting room, just before an interview or even when partying. I never stopped speaking to Him, but in all those conversations, it was me doing all the talking, until now.

It was time for serious life decisions, decisions that could affect the rest of my life and impact me fulfilling my life's purpose. This was big. It was now or never. *Is this why God had intervened? At this moment in time? Would Ryan help me fulfil my life's purpose? Was he part of the plan? What was happening here?* I desperately needed a clear sign for which way to turn, as I now stood at a crossroads. To one side was stability, security and God's will and to the other side was further wandering and exploring of the world – leading to more confusion and later even more despair.

By choosing the wrong path I would have travelled in the direction opposite to where God wanted me to be, leading to more separation from the purpose assigned to me. Revolutionary thought though, I still had the choice. I could have chosen the worldly path but I had been there before. It was bleak and desolate and offered nothing but emptiness which needed to be filled with physical and temporary substitutes and ambitions. The world's way was outside the will of God and I needed to step away from it. Nothing before had worked, I had been searching all this time and finally the Lord intervened.

So, He told me which way to go.

Did I listen?

No!

Masquerading is *pretending to be someone one is not; disguised or passed off as something else.*

For weeks afterwards I tried to continue with my charade of knowing where I was going in life, whether it was my social juggling or applying for any job advertised. I just had to get in that last attempt at figuring things out for myself and by myself. *I knew better. I could do this on my own.* Whether it was geographically or simply anything, maybe something would pop up, maybe.

Ignoring 'my recent message', I was still trying to ride the last leg of this single yet attached persona, even though I was tearing up inside. This internal struggle for peace in the various areas of my life was being smothered under the fabric of prideful lies that had covered me for so long.

I would definitely reach breaking point soon.

And then a few weeks later,

… it happened again.

I heard the voice.

"Go to Ryan," … *what! Again?*

The same words! "Go to Ryan."

This time I remember physically wanting to brush the voice from my shoulder, as if there was a little person sitting on it and I could knock them off with the back of my hand. Obviously, I couldn't have done so because there was no one sitting on my shoulder. But once more, probably a week later, the words came again. The occurrence of these words were coinciding with the period of time when Ryan was asking me to be his girlfriend, but I continued rebuffing him because I was so confused. Deep down I could see myself being married to him but I was so torn with what I thought I wanted. The *world's* allure was still so sparkly. Our connection and longing for one another came so easily so the biggest part of me was keen but the other part was oddly resisting.

I would be going about my normal day while wandering the roads of the Gauteng province in my peach orange vessel and the voice would fill me, "Go to Ryan." It would come audibly and impress on my spirit at regular intervals, but I kept brushing them away.

After about the fourth refusal at his request to be his girlfriend, he consequentially gave me more space than I would have liked – which was completely natural. The phone calls died down and the messaging got less. I then got a sour taste of what it would feel like to be distanced from him.

I couldn't have it. Who was I kidding? I missed him, *and loved him.*

For the word of God *is* living and powerful, and sharper than any two-edged sword, piercing even to the division of soul and spirit, and of joints and marrow, and is a discerner of the thoughts and intents of the heart. – Hebrews 4:12

Eventually, after weeks and weeks, possibly even close to two months of ignoring *the message in the voice*, I finally agreed to Ryan's request and officially became his girlfriend.

And I never heard the voice again. *Thank you, Lord.*

**For I know the thoughts that I think toward you,
says the Lord, thoughts of peace and not of evil, to
give you a future and a hope. – Jeremiah 29:11**

One year later we were engaged, and a year after that we were married.

HOME AT LAST

No sooner was I with Ryan did my insecurities of instability and bewilderment dissipate. I felt safe and secure with him and felt like I finally belonged somewhere. I had found that place I had been driving to. Up and down the thousands of streets and highways of seven major cities for several years. I had finally arrived at my destination: home away from home. Only God knew.

Our wedding day was very special and an opportunity to do this relationship right. We chose to take our first act as husband and wife as partaking *in communion* together. Communion is the sharing of the Eucharist by partaking of the consecrated bread and wine. An action seen as entering into a particularly close relationship with Christ. The following morning: being the first morning as a married couple, we walked down to the river's edge in our dressing gowns and as we arrived at the riverside, we both felt a strong *Peace* meet us. It was as if God was pleased with our new marital status and that what we had done was right in His eyes. We both felt it.

Right from the beginning stages of my relationship with Ryan, the Lord was there, close by. Ready to take my hand and lead me to the man He had planned for me. So even to this day, tough days and good, I hold on to the knowledge that this is the man God led me to. This is the man, above all others, God wanted me to be with. This man with His unwavering integrity and wisdom, solid character and righteous fear of God, the Lord chose Him for me with purpose and led me to Him. Most importantly, I trust in the greater plan for which we are together and feel strengthened to endure any obstacle we face.

After all, it is the Son of God who is the "author and finisher of our faith" (Hebrews 12:12). And just as Christ "endured the cross" (Hebrews 12:12) which brought glory to God, we too must bring glory to God by enduring the struggles that lie not only in marriage, but also in life itself. We must endure. We must fight. We must stand strong. All creation sings Glory to God and marriage is one of His creations, therefore marriage was intended to honour the Creator.

The Lord led me to Ryan, and has been leading me ever since. I suppose that's why the first time I heard the following lyrics, I melted into them and just had to walk down the aisle to this song on my wedding day:

He leadeth me! O blessed thought.

He leadeth me! O blessed thought,
O words with heav'nly comfort fraught;
Whate'er I do, where'er I be,
Still 'tis Christ's hand that leadeth me.

He leadeth me! He leadeth me!
By His own hand He leadeth me;
His faithful follower I would be,
For by His hand He leadeth me.

Sometimes 'mid scenes of deepest gloom,
Sometimes where Eden's bowers bloom,
By waters still, o'er troubled sea,
Still 'tis His hand that leadeth me.

Lord, I would clasp Thy hand in mine,
Nor ever murmur or repine;
Content, whatever lot I see,
Since it is Thou that leadest me.

And when my task on earth is done,
When, by Thy grace, the vict'ry's won,
E'en death's cold wave I will not flee,
Since Thou in triumph leadest me.

Category: Experience of Christ
Subcategory: Following Him
Lyrics: Joseph Henry Gilmore (1834-1918)
Music: William Batchelder Bradbury (1816-1868)
Performed by: Candi Pearsons

Third area pride affected: identity – before

Hollywood lied to me.

All those years, they lied to me.

Film after film, sitcom after sitcom, song after song, media event after media event, one lie at a time. And I bought it. I bought it because it was packaged so attractively, so seductively, so idealistically. I bought it because I had something visual to aspire to. I bought it because it looked like the way to live. I bought it because it was popular. And I bought the lies because I didn't know they were lies.

I am talking about the alluring portrayal of 'the celebrity'. The depicted lifestyle of glitz and glamour, the honeymoon portrayal of relationships, money is everything, success is everything, looks trump everything, prestige is key, status matters, smart cars equal happiness, fashion wins everytime, and climbing the career ladder is all that counts. I was after all of this. I thought that I would be acknowledged in this way. I thought that this representation of life on a screen would give me the answers. I thought that the way they did life was the way to do it. I thought that imitating their behaviour would give me meaning. I thought that imitating their behaviour would give me the identity I had been desperately craving. I thought that I would find my identity.

WHAT IS IDENTITY?

Identity is *the system of belief or framework you identify with or rely on, to provide you with definitions.* Definitions are the bones for meaning. A definition provides the border, a boundary and a limit in which to function. Definitions define and provide the parameters of our identity, in other words, what defines us.

What you believe in and live by is determined by who and what you identify with. Identity therefore tells us how we feel and think about various subject matters, such as, marriage, culture, parenting, gender, schooling, education, religion, politics and worldviews to name but a few. In my case for example, I was searching to identify with the world, which meant I was wanting the world to provide me with definitions to live by, therefore define me. By defining me, I would then be given the meaning, limits and purpose I was craving.

The problem with this is that my foundation of belief was rooted in how the Bible defined things. But I had been searching in the *world's dictionary* to define my life because its definitions were readily available on any screen at any time, as well as visually appealing. I was being pulled between two polar opposites of belief. It is this struggle that resulted in my decade of despair. This is why I felt so torn. Torn between two worlds.

I was wrestling with my Biblical worldview and my earthly desires to live a worldly life. And, they don't mesh. For example: there is a popular American comedy series that was aired during the nineties, and is still often aired today on various channels. The show was a mega hit and won many television awards. So, when I was an impressionable young girl wanting lifestyles to aspire to, a show like that would have influenced me no doubt. Only after watching the show, many many years afterwards and with renewed eyes, did I realise how plainly secular and anti-biblical it was. Within the first eleven minutes of the first pilot episode, the viewer is introduced to fornication, divorce, adultery, homosexuality, blasphemy, infidelity, and promiscuity, and because it's a comedy – the audience laughs, and so are we expected to. These were the messages being distributed via screen, to the comfort of our own homes. And these were the messages that young minds, like myself, were absorbing. This was the dilemma I faced (along with many others).

It took me at least ten years of wandering before I realised what I was wrestling with, and how it had been covered up.

They are not of the world, just as I am
not of the world. – John 17:16
The chapter on identity pauses here for the moment and
will reappear once the covers have been removed,

… continue reading.

PART

TWO

The big reveal – what's really under the cover

For we do not wrestle against flesh and blood, but against principalities, against powers, against the rulers of the darkness of this age, against spiritual *hosts* of wickedness in the heavenly *places*. Therefore take up the whole armour of God, that you may be able to withstand in the evil day, and having done all, to stand. - Ephesians 6:12-13

Cautionary note: the following chapter deals with the subject matter of sin and evil. I am giving notice of this at the onset because this theme can unsettle anyone not familiar with this area of theology, so it's better to be aware of it beforehand.

I know perfectly well how unsettling this topic can be when confronted with material of a supernatural genre, let alone the *dark side* of the supernatural because it was in the very juvenile stages of my journey as a Christian where I experienced this topic first-hand.

The first time I ever came face to face with the presence of an evil spirit, it was so strong and compelling I have never ever forgotten it. The sensation was so confronting that it propelled me to a real and tangible awareness of the spiritual realm and became as real to me as my own body. The experience also gradually unravelled the depths of spiritual gifting and shaped my journey of faith in a way that has surpassed my expectations. This one experience impacted my entire life, so yes – this area of theology is very powerful.

Knowing that there is a spiritual realm that exists concurrent to ours is vital to a full understanding of the truth.

In the interest of pursuing the truth with the aim of sharing the fullness of this message, and most importantly fulfilling the ultimate purpose of this book, this topic must be dealt with. It can't be sugar coated or gently shoved aside because that would be sharing only one third of the truth, and how would that help anybody? Therefore, I stand firmly in saying: what the Bible says about Satan and demons – is completely accurate. Yes, they are real and exist today.

As for you, you were dead in your transgressions and sins, in which you used to live when you followed the ways of this world and of the ruler of the kingdom of the air, the spirit who is now at work in those who are disobedient. All of us also lived among them at one time, gratifying the cravings of our flesh and following its desires and thoughts. – Ephesians 2: 1-3

A warning can seem far-fetched but it is necessary before such a heavy subject matter is discussed because reading about evil is not to be taken lightly at all. There are so many facets to it, all of them horrific but some because of human curiosity can seem intriguing. This intrigue can be dangerous because it is in this moment of curiosity where one can open a door to a demonic influence without even knowing it, the effects of which can be life altering.

I have first-hand experience with this 'dangerous curiosity' and feeling the consequences of being too curious so it is advisable to be cautioned. While lying in bed one night and researching on this very section of the book I started clicking on links to subject areas I'd never before read about, and found myself slightly captivated. These alluring topics were not entirely applicable to the goal of the research but because I was in exploration mode, I didn't think anything of it and thought that because of how strong my faith was I was safe from all threat. But as I read further and further, all the while knowing full well that the more inquisitive I became, the more *charmed* I was getting, something happened midway through an article I was reading. I felt a burning grasp around my neck, as if something was trying to choke me. I knew the sensation was real because I grabbed my neck instantly and started rubbing at my skin to remove it. At this feeling I promptly threw my phone down and began praying because I knew exactly what it was.

This is exactly why it is imperative not to be taken unawares and be caught off guard. It is in moments like this that affirm the reality of the spiritual realm, whether you like it or not.

We are not only living existences in flesh but spiritual existences too. Therefore, this chapter is vital, not only because it has implications for this earthly life but also because it has implications for the life hereafter.

Therefore take up the whole armour of God, that you may be able to withstand in the evil day, and having done all, to stand.

Stand therefore, having girded your waist with truth, having put on the breastplate of righteousness, and having shod your feet

with the preparation of the gospel of peace; above all, taking the shield of faith with which you will be able to quench all the fiery darts of the wicked one. And take the helmet of salvation, and the sword of the Spirit, which is the word of God; praying always with all prayer and supplication in the Spirit, being watchful to this end with all perseverance and supplication for all the saints.
— Ephesians 6:13-18

BEING AWARE

The first step in fighting a battle is determining who your adversary is - who your enemy is? Since it is always best to prepare for a potential battle then to be caught unarmed, if you are in denial about the existence of Satan you are already unarmed. You have been misled (by whatever unbelief you have, or denomination you belong to) because he is just as real as the coffee you're drinking. Pretending that Satan doesn't exist, doesn't make him unreal. It also doesn't send him away either. Pretending that the devil – "Your adversary the devil walks about like a roaring lion, seeking whom he may devour" (1 Peter 5:8) - isn't trying to sneak his way into your marriage, your family, your home and your life, is useless. Pretending that he is not trying to lead you away from God's will for your life means that you have been deceived. Feeling unphased about this aspect of the truth, or being in denial of it, just leaves you open to an attack or influence you are not even aware could be possible. It also leaves you open to believing half-truths and lies because you aren't even aware of what the truth really is, so how will you know when you have been blindly fed a false one?

Reading about dark forces and wickedness can dot your mind with disturbing thoughts and before you know it, warped ideas slip into your mind and begin twisting your normally good-natured perspective on things - so be very vigilant. It's important to know that when this happens what it is. It is also important to guard against unnecessary curiosity, keep on the subject and don't stray too far off. Be careful, you are only human. This is why you must pray for protection by putting on the full armour of God as found in the book of Ephesians.

During the time of writing this section of the chapter, I thankfully knew that I could turn to prayer and Christian counsel for guidance. After several days of these obscure thoughts, I contacted a trusted mentor, a wise and trusted woman who was well respected in our church community. At the age of eighty-three her and I shared the deep yearning we have for the Lord and could talk for great lengths about Scripture, Biblical history, our feelings, insecurities and prayers. I really treasured this very special relationship and knew that she would listen fully without judgement when I contacted her. After I told her what I had been experiencing and that I had been researching the origin of sin which opened up material on evil, the cheerfulness in her voice dropped to concern which immediately led her to begin praying for me over the phone. She then told me something I now keep with me when I am feeling despondent in times such as these. "You are victorious because Christ is victorious, don't give the enemy any power. The name of Jesus is above all other names and He has the authority over any stronghold."

But thanks be to God, who gives us the victory through our Lord Jesus Christ. – 1 Corinthians 15:57

Therefore God also has highly exalted Him and given Him the name which is above every name, that at the name of Jesus every knee should bow, of those in heaven, and of those on earth, and of those under the earth, and *that* every tongue should confess that Jesus Christ *is* Lord, to the glory of God the Father. – Philippians 2:9-11

Without even realising it, one can unknowingly open a door for evil influences to enter your life through sinful acts. But because this book is written for the glory of God with the aim of pointing the reader to the testimony of Christ, not distract, lead astray or steer away from it, with the Lord's help, whatever topic is covered may it lead the reader to the truth.

Then some of the itinerant Jewish exorcists took it upon themselves to call the name of the Lord Jesus over those who had evil spirits, saying, "We exorcise you by the Jesus whom Paul preaches." Also there were seven sons of Sceva, a Jewish chief priest, who did so.

And the evil spirit answered and said, "Jesus I know, and Paul I know; but who are you?"

Then the man in whom the evil spirit was leaped on them, overpowered them, and prevailed against them, so that they fled out of that house naked and wounded. This became known both to all Jews and Greeks dwelling in Ephesus; and fear fell on them all, and the name of the Lord Jesus was magnified. And many who had believed came confessing and telling their deeds. Also, many of those who had practiced magic brought their books together and burned *them* in the sight of all. And they counted up the value of them, and *it* totalled fifty thousand *pieces* of silver. So the word of the Lord grew mightily and prevailed. – Acts 19:13 – 20

A LIFE CHANGING ENCOUNTER

At seventeen-years-old, in the year 2000, I travelled with my family to Thailand for a two-and-a-half-week holiday during the month of December. While we were there as tourists, we signed up to tour a section of a large river and nearby snake and monkey park via boat. Just before disembarking the boat after crossing the river, the tour guide mentioned that this area was notorious for its sex slavery. It was then that something happened, something not of this physical world.

As bright as the sun shines on a totally clear day, what I am about to share with you was just as obvious.

The very second my foot touched the jetty of that island, was the very second I was hit. I was hit with a wall of evil. *A wall of evil spirits.*

I had never ever experienced anything like this before, but when it happened, I immediately recognised what it was. Even with my very limited to almost no teaching in this area, the realisation of what it was struck me instantly. It felt as if there was conflict, a battle going on around me.

The best way to describe the physical sensation is in terms of drastic temperature change. When you open the door to a sauna at the gym and that thick wave of steamy heat from inside the sauna room hits your cooler body. It was that intense. It was that tangible.

It was also the same feeling one gets when stepping into an icy cold walk-in refrigerator. It's the drastic immediate change from one state to the next that best describes the sensation I experienced. The marked contrast in feeling warm one second and icy cold the next illustrates the intensity of what occurred. As strong as the force was on that day on the jetty it was not visible to the naked eye because it was not of this world, but rather of another one which exists concurrently to the one we are all currently living.

With my limited understanding and experience of the supernatural, I suppose that my *clean / light / Godly / reborn* spirit - *the Holy Spirit* - inside of me, came into conflict with the evil ones that were present on the island and that it is why I felt such a compelling force against me. Even the monkeys at the snake park were squealing uncontrollably and yelping nonstop. I am not quite sure why the animals were behaving in this abnormal way but I can only assume that because of their heightened sensory capabilities they detected an irregularity on another level. Animals can definitely sense a threatening environment very keenly, so their behaviour on the day we were there makes sense. To this day, I will never ever forget this incident, my first but not last encounter with *spiritual warfare*.

The reason I am sharing this is to give witness to the spiritual realm. There is a spiritual world that is real, just as everything around you exists, whether you understand it or not. So, take cognisance of this knowledge and realise that what is contained in the Bible, is real.

There are diversities of gifts, but the same Spirit. There are differences of ministries, but the same Lord. And there are diversities of activities, but it is the same God who works all in all. But the manifestation of the Spirit is given to each one for the profit *of all:* for to one is given the word of wisdom through the Spirit, to another the word of knowledge through the same Spirit, to another faith by the same Spirit, to another gifts of healings by the same Spirit, to another the working of miracles, to another prophecy, to another discerning of spirits, to another *different* kinds of tongues, to another the interpretation of tongues. But one and the same Spirit works all these things, distributing to each one individually as He wills. – 1 Corinthians 12: 4-11

SPIRITUAL GIFTING

One of the privileges of being given the opportunity to write about one's testimony is that you have a time slot in which to learn more on a myriad of relevant topics because you are constantly reading up on the subject you're writing about. So, when I came to the point of writing about the spiritual confrontation I had in Thailand on the jetty, I did some digging on whether some Christians are more prone to 'sensing the supernatural' than other Christians. And then I found it. I found it in the place where I should have looked a decade-and-a-half before

before – the Bible. Only Scripture can fully equip humanity with a clear demonstration of God's intention for the human race, both the Old and New Testament. No other writings are as authoritative or obligatory for the truth to be realised. All Scripture is "God-breathed" and so is sufficient.

The answer then as to why I feel so 'spiritually aware', according to 1 Corinthians 12:4-11, is because I have probably been given the spiritual gift to do so. Finally noticing this gives me peace but at the same time liberates me because I finally have an answer to the decade-and-a-half long question as to why I experienced what I did that day in Thailand. Even though I didn't have the head knowledge of what happened that day, the experience shows that the Holy Spirit works beyond our human capabilities and understanding.

Christians, in general (and I speak generally), can be quite lax sometimes in formally studying the Bible. Some of us can take a very *slow* approach to reading this library of books from beginning to end, if ever, and do a lot of book and passage hopping. Even though I was only seventeen, I should have known more about 'gifting'. We really ought to be studying the word of God with triumphant gusto and know it with heartfelt sincerity and conviction as "All Scripture *is* given by inspiration of God, and *is* profitable for doctrine, for reproof, for correction, for instruction in righteousness, that the man of God may be complete, thoroughly equipped for every good work" (2 Timothy 3: 16-17). The time and money spent studying towards one's career should match the effort spent studying scripture. The Bible after all is the most valuable and significant book there is. It is both historical and supernatural.

Following on from my admission of guilt of not knowing the relevant Scripture on *gifting,* I can hopefully now move on to the work God has purposed for me. Absolutely and without doubt this is the biggest motivation in my life, to share with others the truths He has allowed me to witness. My deepest hope is for the Lord to use me wherever He needs me with whatever gifting He has bestowed on me - nothing would bring me greater joy.

A relationship with God is so real that you can actually feel the presence of His Spirit in moments of His choosing. Even though the presence of His Spirit has come to me in different ways at various times, I know it is from Him because the experience is intimate, powerfully peaceful and dramatically reassuring. He is the One that chooses the experience for this affirmation.

The following experiences are moments of supernatural communication that are etched in my memory bank.

MEMORABLE MOMENTS OF COMMUNICATION

The final exam of my Languages and Literature degree was scheduled for a Monday morning at half-past-eight so I spent the whole weekend by myself in order to prepare for it. Being the final exam, I felt an added pressure to pass it, as failing would have delayed my graduation by a whole six months. On the morning of the exam everything was going as planned and running as per normal when suddenly something happened, something I had never experienced before. *It's interesting how these spiritual affirmations were coming through in various ways.*

While sitting on the sofa in the lounge and brushing my daughter's hair, *a concentrated washing of peace poured over me.* The feeling was the same as having a bucket of water being gently poured over your head by someone standing in front of you. Just as the water would have soaked you entirely, I felt the same way. I felt drenched in a *rich concentrated undiluted outpouring of peace.* It was sensational and the sensation was unmatched to anything I have ever felt before - it was glorious. *The pouring* didn't continue for long, it was brief but completely unforgettable. Little did I realise in that moment what a drastic impact that outpouring would mean for me later that same morning.

Once seated in the exam hall a while after that and waiting in anticipation for my paper to arrive, I strangely didn't have the urge to pray for my imminent examination as I normally would have. But what I did have was the bizarre prompting to pray for something else. Right here occurs another *memorable moment* because this had never happened before either.

I had the prompting to pray for "my daughter's husband".

Seriously? Right now? Minutes before my exam I am urged to pray for something I have never even thought of … seriously. I am just about to write the final exam of my degree and this is what I am guided to pray for. I can't believe it. I couldn't believe it. Firstly, because this had never before crossed my mind, especially in this kind of situation and secondly, my daughter was only two years old. *Why is God leading me to pray for her husband, she is nowhere near getting married, she is barely out of nappies.*

With the looming stress of my approaching exam paper being carried down the row towards me, I think I may have uttered a thought, barely even a prayer for this, definitely nothing worthy to influence anything that might have occurred elsewhere that morning (at least I would imagine). However, since this occurrence though I have prayed for both my children's spouses. What an astonishing request though at such an inopportune time (for me at least). The whole thing just caught me off guard.

In reflecting about this moment: prayer is obviously something far greater than we perceive it to be. It obviously has an influence in a realm beyond our physical awareness and affects circumstances beyond our human comprehension for it to mean anything. It must do considering that even Jesus, the Son of God, prayed.

Why pray if there is no effect or possible change in outcome to be expected? That morning the Holy Spirit prompted me to pray for someone I did not even know. Why? What would the purpose of that be if there was nothing my words could have influenced? Where were the words going? Who was hearing the words? Who or what would have been influenced by the mere words in my prayer? What is prayer then ... really? It is more than what we realise?

But ...

this memorable moment doesn't stop here ...

As I was handed the exam paper, I quickly glanced at the first question and my heart descended into my stomach. My hands immediately went numb and I'm sure the colour drained from my face as my heart rate quickened. In one quick glimpse at the paper, I realised I had focussed entirely on the wrong area of work and therefore wasn't properly prepared at all.

Had I really spent the entire weekend studying in vain? Why had I done this to myself? What a waste! I really don't want to fail this exam. This is so stupid of me! I really wanted to finish my course this semester and not delay it for another six months. I can't believe I have done this. What have I done; this is my last exam? Come on Candace, how could you let this happen? I think I'm just going to get up and walk out of here, even though I have never done that before either. But I am feeling so overwhelmed at the moment. I honestly just feel like going to the car and sobbing my eyes out.

But wait a minute.

What happened earlier this morning?

What ACTUALLY happened earlier this morning? What was that?

What was that extraordinary and unexpected experience I had in the lounge?

What was that extraordinary outpouring of peace I experienced?

What was the purpose of it? What did it mean? Why this morning in particular? It couldn't have just been coincidence, on today of all days, nothing with God is only coincidence. What was that outpouring of Peace – and why today?

Wait a minute!

Maybe God was preparing me for the dilemma I am facing right now in this exam hall? He must have been telling me something. I think He was demonstrating to me that He knew this was going to happen and that I'd be facing this decision at my desk right now. I think, the Peace he poured over me was a sign that He is with me and it signifies that everything is going to be okay. I think I need to write this exam.

God had prepared me for that moment. He knew that I would face that decision, He saw it coming before I ever did. He poured *His Peace* over me earlier that morning to demonstrate His presence, as well as His plan, and He did it that morning of all mornings. On the morning I would face a decision whether to hand my exam paper in and walk out or give the paper a second glance: a decision that would cost me six months.

But … I must first believe it.

I must first trust this.

I must first trust that what happened, is what I am sure happened.

I must first trust Him.

Okay ... I believe that what happened was real and was from You Lord, I prayed.

I trust you Lord.

I'm letting go!

... here goes!

Taking a deep breathe I took hold of the exam paper once more, wiped the glum look from my face and said to myself, "Candace, you can do this, you must know something about this area of work. Take one question at a time and write what you know." So, I did.

I didn't fail the exam as I'd dreaded but instead passed with a whopping seventy-two percent missing a distinction by only three percent.

Passing the exam that day enabled me to use the remaining six months of the year to begin writing this book, a book that would give me the opportunity to testify about my walk with the Lord.

A continuous personal prayer of mine has always been: "Lord use me, make me an instrument."

PONDERING IN MY CAR

As I write this very sentence it has been roughly two-and-a-half years since starting this book. I am currently sitting in my car in an underground parking lot at the local shopping centre because this is a place where I can really concentrate on my writing because there is nothing around me to divert my attention. With no access to Wi-Fi, I am not drawn to going online and getting distracted. Here in the passenger seat, I can write without interference. With only the occasional glance at a passing shopper, it's become a very productive place for writing and polishing up this final draft.

Scrolling back to the pages to when I began writing and back to the ones written just recently, I get a sense of how God has been leading me to this very point. A point where I need to be before He can take me to the next step. *I am ready Lord!* It moves me to think about why I am sitting in this car in the first place and what I am busy doing: opening up truthfully so that others may benefit from my vulnerability and so be encouraged to search for and discover the *Truth* for themselves and then receive it. My deepest desire is for unbelievers to be led to the LORD through my journey and for believers to be strengthened in theirs.

The Lord has graciously allowed me to open up tiny secrets of the Kingdom of Heaven in order to better equip me for this next chapter. As I write and edit the last pages, I feel inspired to take on the next chapter of what I hope to be His will for my life.

For this *is* good and acceptable in the sight of God our Saviour, who desires all men to be saved and to come to the knowledge of the truth. – 1 Timothy 2:3-4

GOING RIGHT BACK TO THE BEGINNING

Why I provided a warning, and why the first two attempts at writing this book failed miserably, and why this version turned into something completely different. It was because this version of the book wasn't ready to be written initially. Plainly - because the writer wasn't ready. The writer wasn't ready to write the full message. As a *servant* of the

Lord, I was not developed enough and so like undercooked pasta, my words would have been awful to digest. The words, my approach to the subject matter, the motive, the message (if any), the structure and the objective that I would have used in the first two versions of the book would not have brought justice to the journey I have walked with the Lord and would have simply tried to share what happened in my life from purely my perspective. When in fact this book was never going to be about me, it was always going to be about Him. My life was never going to be about me, it was always going to be about Him. The Lord not only closed the doors on those two versions, He slammed them shut.

This book was never going to be about me, it was always going to be about Him.

My life was never going to about me, it was always going to be about Him.

A regular prayer of mine, and one of the most effective: "Lord God, please open the doors You want opened, and close the doors You want closed."

I hadn't yet developed into the messenger that would do justice to the journey. This book is for Him and the message needs to be for His Glory. It has also been written to show that through my weaknesses, His strength can be magnified.

My grace is sufficient for you, for My strength is made perfect in weakness. – 2 Corinthians 12: 7-10

By the time this version (the one you're reading) was ready to be written, I would have asked Him to lead me through the writing and only He could have known that I would have done so. Only He would have known whether I was at this point in my journey of faith, the point where I needed to be to tell the whole story, the point where I had realised that I was never living for my purpose but rather to fulfil God's purpose for me. This is the point where I needed to be.

Praise the LORD, O my soul!
While I live I will praise the LORD;
I will sing praises to my God while I
have my being. – Psalm 146:1-2

The first two drafts of the book would have told my story and would only have shared my struggles from a purely human view of life on earth. But I see now as I type these words that I was always meant to share *the whole story*. So, third time round here I am writing solely for the glory of His Holy Name and for the *Truth* and only through the marvel that is God's timing, it is happening.

If anyone speaks, let him speak as the oracles of God. If anyone ministers, let him do it as with the ability which God supplies, that in all things God may be glorified through Jesus Christ, to whom belong the glory and the dominion forever and ever. Amen. – 1 Peter 4:11

WHERE TO START?

The section that follows is actually the first piece of the book that was written and I'll tell you why. When I finally decided that I was going to give the book a real go, after the duo of doomed literature. I sat before an open blank MS Word document and prayed. For the first time since I had the urge to share my journey at all, I actually prayed about it. Never before with the previous two versions did I ever stop to pray or think to pray because I was doing it for me. So, this time, I asked the Lord to guide me through every page and keep me focused on the true message. I then asked the Lord to tell me what the first chapter should be on and how I should begin the book.

Then the Spirit entered me when He spoke to me, and set me on my feet; and I heard Him who spoke to me. – Ezekiel 2:2

And then it came,

- another memorable moment -

in a clear affirmation to my being … the answer flowed into my awareness with these words, "Pride" - the first chapter must be about pride. The book must begin at pride because that is where it all began.

I was gobsmacked. Wow! *Thank you, Lord, for this answer.* Without this answer I had nowhere to start. *Amazing!*

In stunned silence, I began to research. And this is what I discovered.

GOING RIGHT BACK TO BEFORE EDEN

Growing up with a foundation in church life rooted my understanding that the Bible is the Word of God, something I am very grateful for receiving as a young child. This training and teaching I received as a child was invaluable as it cemented my belief in God. Although I am exceedingly grateful for the childhood church training I received, if it had just been left there, I would not have grown to the extent I have. Thankfully the Lord touched me in various ways, through people and through His Holy Spirit, causing me to seek Him more earnestly. I firmly believe that each one of us must endeavour to pursue their Saviour personally. One cannot rely on anyone else to seek and find the *Truth* for you. Each one must know for certain who Jesus is.

Once I started studying the Bible for myself, I realised how much I didn't know. For example: I had never before studied or even touched on the *origin of sin* and *pride*. I had no idea what pride was. And this is where we are now.

It is at this point where the warning note to reader I mentioned previously is intended. It is here where I begin unpacking *the whole story*, it is here that I begin unpacking 'pride' and its ugly face.

Pride goes before destruction, And a haughty spirit before a fall.
- Proverbs 16:18

Ever come across the popular saying, "Pride comes before a fall". I had, but I never knew that it actually came from the Bible. In all my years I thought it was a secular maxim and was amazed to discover during my research on pride that it actually originates from the Biblical book of Proverbs. I also discovered that pride doesn't actually come before the fall, it comes before destruction, a haughty spirit is what comes before the fall. Synonyms for haughty are arrogant, disdainful, proud, vain, conceited, condescending, egotistical, full-of-oneself, above oneself and self-important – it is these feelings then that cause you to fall.

I also then discovered that I knew very little to nothing about pride in terms of Biblical truth, and its real place in the world. Just 'Google' pride and see what pops up, certainly not the definition of pride I was after. I will also sheepishly admit that I never really understood in the slightest way what pride is and how God responds to it until I began researching for this chapter. I also never realised that pride goes way beyond our human grasp of what it could be or even mean, it stretches far beyond our everyday comprehension. There is a great deal of literature on pride, from the Holy Scriptures to Greek philosophy, from psychology to art, and most resources lead pride to the same origin: 'the self'. Which is *the* 'preoccupation or obsession with the self', self-love, and self-exaltation.

The word 'self' is defined according to the Advanced Oxford Dictionary as *a person's essential being that distinguishes them from others, especially considered as the object of introspection or reflexive action*. In the research I conducted, 'the self' or 'the preoccupation with the self' is a difficult concept to understand if we do not have a point of reference.

What does this mean? The preoccupation with self.

Where did this 'preoccupation with the self' begin and this overbearing connection with oneself originate because the world is riddled with it? In fact, where did anything originate? Yes, the age-old question, why are we here, where did it all begin? Even though this is not the subject we are discussing at the moment, it does enhance the inevitable outcome of this discussion. When building a house, the foundation determines the end structure, so let's start there - at the foundation. What happens in the beginning determines the end product and so when we want to find what we're looking for; it is best to start at the beginning.

The beginning for me is the beginning with God and so now I turn to the Word of God for all answers. It is written in Genesis 1:1 that, "In the beginning God created the heavens and the earth." This is the first Biblical statement that demonstrates that God was not created. He was the creator who was always there, omnipotent and eternal. He is the Alpha and the Omega (the beginning and the end) and had *life* before the heavens and the earth. This first Biblical statement further tells us that before creation, God was *in time of His own*. Mankind will never comprehend the length or breadth of time that existed before the earth was formed because to God "One day is like a thousand years and a thousand years is like one day" (2 Peter 3:8). God is also not bound by time, space and matter like we are.

What is really fascinating and relevant to the study about pride is the period in time when God was creating the heavens and the earth.

Obviously, we can't be certain of what happened during this time but we can use Scripture to give us a reasonable idea. When I started unpacking all of this, I was blown away at what I discovered for the very first time.

After probing deeper into the topic on pride, it turns out that the events that took place before and during creation are actually essential to this study. The events that took place before man provide the leading answers to the many question's humans have about why the world is the way it is, evil, suffering and its place in the world.

When I started out compiling this book, I never intended for there to be sections where research was required because I had planned for it to relay only my version of events during my decade of despair but the Lord has taken me further than that decade and led me beyond that. I thought I'd only be writing about what happened to me in high school and so on, but this is how the story has unfolded, so here goes.

As I have been led, these theological areas have emerged and so must be clarified in order for the full story to surface. The purpose of this book has always been to give the reader the whole story anyway, be led where the Lord leads me and hopefully lead the reader to the *Truth*. If this means expanding on areas with further evidence, then it must be done. Even though we could never determine exact dates in God's timeline, the following discussion is critical in better trying to grasp pride. In all my years – I had never delved into pride – the very origin of sin.

BEFORE HUMANS

In the beginning God created the heavens and the earth. The earth was without form, and void; and darkness was on the face of the deep. And the Spirit of God was hovering over the face of the waters. – Genesis 1:1-2

In a time before the creation of the earth, God *was* and *is eternally present*. Yes, this I can grasp easily, God is before everything else. Then what? What came next? And this was interesting to me. According to the book of Job, the angels were actually "worshipping God" (Job 38:4-7) during the creation of the world, therefore the angels existed prior, for how long no human knows, to the creation of the world.

Job 38:4-7

"Where were you when I laid the foundations of the earth?
Tell Me, if you have understanding.
Who determined its measurements?
Surely you know!
Or who stretched the line upon it?
To what were its foundations fastened?
Or who laid its cornerstone,
When the morning stars sang together,
And all the sons of God shouted for joy?"

In this passage, God is asking Job a series of questions that no human could possibly answer. The sons of God whom the Lord speaks of in this passage were the angels. "Star" is also used to refer to angels in the Bible.

Trying to determine exactly when God created the angels is impossible to us because the Bible isn't explicit about it and anything that God did "before the foundation of the world" puts the event outside human time itself anyway. All we have to know is that God created angels in a time before earth and man, the time factor is of no consequence. I personally understand the Bible as the message from God to humans which is why it doesn't focus extensively on areas not relating to the relationship between God and humans. Strong evidence of this is that the book of Genesis handles the entire creation of the universe within the first few verses and then quickly moves onto the creation of man. The Bible is a library of books from God to man, specifically demonstrating God's desire to be reconciled with *fallen man*.

Thankfully, there is evidence throughout the Bible on the existence and activities of angels, as well as material on what happened before man was formed. This helps to better comprehend the structure of God's Kingdom, hierarchy and our human position in it. Just like man and any other creature on earth, angels were also created with purpose. Below are a few of the purposeful responsibilities that angels undertake:

They worship God

Psalm 148: 1-2
> Praise the LORD from the heavens;
> Praise Him in the heights!
> Praise Him, all His angels;
> Praise Him, all His hosts!

Hebrews 1:6
> But when He again brings the firstborn into the world, He says:
> "Let all the angels of God worship Him."

Isaiah 6:1-3
> In the year that King Uzziah died, I saw the Lord sitting on a throne, high and lifted up, and the train of His robe filled the temple. Above it stood seraphim; each one had six wings: with two he covered his face, with two he covered his feet, and with two he flew. And one cried to another and said:
> "Holy, holy, holy is the LORD of hosts;
> The whole earth is full of His glory!"

They rejoice in what God does

Luke 15:10

> In the same way, I tell you, there is joy in the presence of the angels of God over one sinner who repents.

Luke 2:13-14

> And suddenly there was with the angel a multitude of the heavenly host praising God and saying:
> "Glory to God in the highest,
> And on earth peace, goodwill toward men!"

They appear before God

Job 1:6

> Now there was a day when the sons of God came to present themselves before the LORD, ..."

They observe Christian order, work, and suffering:

Acts 12:5-8

> Peter was therefore kept in prison, but constant prayer was offered to God for him by the church. And when Herod was about to bring him out, that night Peter was sleeping, bound with two chains between two soldiers; and the guards before the door were keeping the prison. Now behold, an angel of the Lord stood by him, and a light shone in the prison; and he struck Peter on the side and raised him up, saying, "Arise quickly!" And his chains fell off his hands. Then the angel said to him, "Gird yourself and tie on your sandals"; and so he did. And he said to him, "Put on your garment and follow me."

Angels are also instruments of God's judgment, they aid in bringing people to Christ, are messengers, serve God, bring answers to prayer, encourage in times of danger, they care for the righteous at the time of death, they are ministering spirits, and are sent forth to minister for those who will inherit salvation.

It is the following three characteristics of angels though that is most relevant for the purpose of this specific study on pride:

expressing emotion,
possessing intelligence,
and exercising free will.

So just like humans, angels exercise free will - therefore they too have the ability of choice. Right now, you may be confused, just as I was, as to why we are discoursing on angels when the subject is pride. Well, little did I know before I started my research on this subject area, was that the subject of angels and pride are connected.

Why you ask, how can they possibly be associated? I'll gladly explain, not only because this subject area completely intrigues me but because it's absolutely vital to unpacking the answer to the age-old question, "what is as the root of all evil?"

ANGELS

Let's get started.

Name

Amongst the angels whom the Lord created, was an angel named Lucifer. He was later named Satan and is also known as the devil. Lucifer was Satan's name as an angel, it appears in Isaiah 14:12, "O Lucifer, son of the morning!"

Character

In the passage below, the prophet Ezekiel was sent by God to make a proclamation against the King of Tyre regarding his aggressively growing pride. The city of Tyre was well known for acquiring wealth by exploiting its neighbours using its strategic geographical location, as well as harbouring sexual immorality and religious idolatry.

Ezekiel 27:1-4

The word of the LORD came again to me, saying,
"Now, son of man, take up a lamentation for Tyre, and say to Tyre, 'You who are situated at the entrance of the sea, merchant of the peoples on many coastlands, thus says the Lord GOD:

"O Tyre, you have said,
'I am perfect in beauty.'
Your borders are in the midst of the seas.
Your builders have perfected your beauty."

In the passage below, the characteristics of the King of Tyre are likened to that of Lucifer's. At first glance the passage in Ezekiel refers only to the human king of a city but as one analyses further, we see how this passage actually references Lucifer/Satan. We note this because in no way could this earthly king possess the qualities to be "in Eden, the garden of God", or be "the anointed cherub (angel) who covers," or be "on the holy mountain of God." Therefore, most Biblical interpreters are confident in saying that this passage is a dual prophecy, likening the characteristics of the king of Tyre to the characteristics of Lucifer.

Ezekiel 28:1-19

The word of the LORD came to me again, saying, "Son of man, say to the prince of Tyre, 'Thus says the Lord GOD:

"Because your heart is lifted up,
And you say, 'I am a god,

I sit in the seat of gods,
In the midst of the seas,'
Yet you are a man, and not a god,
Though you set your heart as the heart of a god
(Behold, you are wiser than Daniel!
There is no secret that can be hidden from you!
With your wisdom and your understanding
You have gained riches for yourself,
And gathered gold and silver into your treasuries;
By your great wisdom in trade you have increased your riches,
And your heart is lifted up because of your riches),"

'Therefore thus says the Lord GOD:

"Because you have set your heart as the heart of a god,
Behold, therefore, I will bring strangers against you,
The most terrible of the nations;
And they shall draw their swords against the beauty of your wisdom,
And defile your splendour.
They shall throw you down into the Pit,
And you shall die the death of the slain
In the midst of the seas.
"Will you still say before him who slays you,
'I am a god'?
But you shall be a man, and not a god,
In the hand of him who slays you.
You shall die the death of the uncircumcised
By the hand of aliens;
For I have spoken," says the Lord GOD."

Moreover the word of the LORD came to me, saying, "Son of man,
take up a lamentation for the king of Tyre, and say to him, 'Thus says
the Lord GOD:

"You were the seal of perfection,
Full of wisdom and perfect in beauty.
You were in Eden, the garden of God;
Every precious stone was your covering:
The sardius, topaz, and diamond,

Beryl, onyx, and jasper,
Sapphire, turquoise, and emerald with gold.
The workmanship of your timbrels and pipes
Was prepared for you on the day you were created.

"You were the anointed cherub who covers;
I established you;
You were on the holy mountain of God;
You walked back and forth in the midst of fiery stones.
You were perfect in your ways from the day you were created,
Till iniquity was found in you.

"By the abundance of your trading
You became filled with violence within,
And you sinned;
Therefore I cast you as a profane thing
Out of the mountain of God;
And I destroyed you, O covering cherub,
From the midst of the fiery stones.

"Your heart was lifted up because of your beauty;
You corrupted your wisdom for the sake of your splendor;
I cast you to the ground,
I laid you before kings,
That they might gaze at you.

"You defiled your sanctuaries
By the multitude of your iniquities,
By the iniquity of your trading;
Therefore I brought fire from your midst;
It devoured you,
And I turned you to ashes upon the earth
In the sight of all who saw you.
All who knew you among the peoples are astonished at you;
You have become a horror,
And shall be no more forever."

In the passage above, the book of Ezekiel writes about the casting of
Lucifer from heaven.

Two very important questions that emerge for me are: firstly, why was Lucifer cast out of heaven, and secondly, what would cause God to cast out one of His angels?

Have you ever thought about this? *I hadn't.*

Part of this answer is found in the Old Testament book of Isaiah 14:12-15,

"How you are fallen from heaven,
O Lucifer, son of the morning!
How you are cut down to the ground,
You who weakened the nations!
For you have said in your heart:
'I will ascend into heaven,
I will exalt my throne above the stars of God;
I will also sit on the mount of the congregation
On the farthest sides of the north;
I will ascend above the heights of the clouds,
I will be like the Most High."

Lucifer's banishment was a direct result of his self-exaltation that manifested through pride: the first sin – "not a novice, lest being puffed up with pride he fall into the *same* condemnation as the devil" (1 Timothy 3:6). Motivated by the pride he had for his own beauty, position and wisdom, Lucifer desired to be greater than and/or equal to God. He desired to be exalted and honoured just like God was. He challenged the authority and supremacy of God and determined that it was by his own doing he was who he was, giving no glory to God. He felt that he didn't need Him and forgot all about His Creator. He had also forgotten who God was and had forgotten to fear God.

He who sins is of the devil, for the devil has sinned from the beginning. - 1 John 3:8

Let this be a lesson to each one of us, pride will put you outside the will of God and outside His presence. Let your pride not be your eternal downfall.

Only a humble heart will seek repentance and ask for forgiveness for being outside the will of God because it is in humility where we realise who we are in relation to God: subordinate. We are not equal to or greater than God, and never will be. As creatures, we are created to glorify and bring praise to the Creator. Only through humility can we even think of pleasing Him.

When pride comes, then comes shame;
But with the humble *is* wisdom. – Proverbs 11:2

Blessed *are* those who do His commandments, that they may have the right to the tree of life, and may enter through the gates into the city. But outside *are* dogs and sorcerers and sexually immoral and murderers and idolaters, and whoever loves and practices a lie. – Revelations 22:14-15

A PICTURE WORTH A THOUSAND WORDS

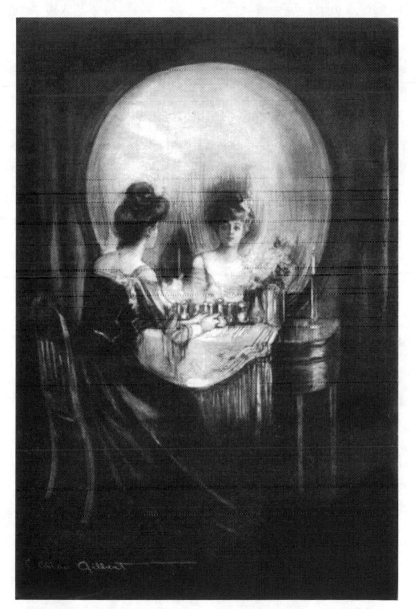

All is vanity (1892), Charles Allan Gilbert (1873 – 1929)

Charles Allan Gilbert is especially remembered for a widely published drawing (a memento mori or vanitas) titled *All Is Vanity*. The drawing cleverly portrays a double image (or visual pun) that when viewed from a distance appears to be a human skull but at a closer look actually reveals a woman admiring her beauty. The title is also a pun, as this type of dressing-table is commonly known as a vanity.

The phrase "All is vanity" is taken from the Biblical book of Ecclesiastes 1:2, "Vanity of vanities, says the Preacher; Vanity of vanities, all is vanity" and refers to the vanity and pride of humans. In art, the concept of vanity is usually portrayed by a woman preoccupied with her beauty. And art that depicts a human skull as a focal point is called a *memento mori* (Latin for "remember you will die"), a work that reminds humans of their mortality.

AT THE ROOT OF EVIL

We don't know this for sure because there is no scripture as corroboration, but there is secondary opinion by Biblical scholars suggesting that Lucifer's rise to rebellion might also have demonstrated during 'creation week'. This was when God created the universe and Lucifer witnessed how "good" it was (Genesis 1:3). The handiwork of God caused Lucifer to revolt because he had so much pride in him*self* that He couldn't stand to see God so honoured. Because God had created something so beautiful, which displayed His awesome power, supremacy and creativity, and was praised for His work by the angels, Lucifer's arrogant self-absorbed nature led him to rebel.

Possibly to back the theory that this revolt occurred during 'the creation of the world' is the following extract from the book of Revelations, "the accuser of our brethren is cast down, which accused them before our God day and night" (Revelations 12:10).

Weren't day and night only in existence during *God's week* of creation?

The purpose of this argument is for us to see how evil, present in the world today, actually came to be here in the first place.

FROM HEAVEN TO EARTH

God's judgement against Lucifer triggered a battle in heaven, as is written in Revelations 12:7-12.

"And war broke out in heaven: Michael and his angels fought with the dragon; and the dragon and his angels fought, but they did not prevail, nor was a place found for them in heaven any longer. So the great dragon was cast out, that serpent of old, called the Devil and Satan, who deceives the whole world; he was cast to the earth, and his angels were cast out with him.

Then I heard a loud voice saying in heaven, "Now salvation, and strength, and the kingdom of our God, and the power of His Christ have come, for the accuser of our brethren, who accused them before our God day and night, has been cast down. And they overcame him by the blood of the Lamb and by the word of their testimony, and they did not love their lives to the death. Therefore rejoice, O heavens, and you who dwell in them! Woe to the inhabitants of the earth and the sea! For the devil has come down to you, having great wrath, because he knows that he has a short time."

THE FALL OF SATAN » THE FALL OF MAN

Now the serpent was more cunning than any beast of the field which the LORD God had made. And he said to the woman, "Has God indeed said, 'You shall not eat of every tree of the garden'?"

And the woman said to the serpent, "We may eat the fruit of the trees of the garden; but of the fruit of the tree which *is* in the midst of the garden, God has said, 'You shall not eat it, nor shall you touch it, lest you die.'"

Then the serpent said to the woman, "You will not surely die. For God knows that in the day you eat of it your eyes will be opened, and you will be like God, knowing good and evil. – Genesis 3:1-5

At the time when Satan approached Eve, both her and Adam were pure. Pure as innocent and naïve children, "naked" and "not ashamed" (Genesis 2:25). They were "holy, unblemished" and "blameless" in His presence" (Colossians 1:22), therefore God Himself was able to walk in the Garden because only what is blameless and *clean* can be in His presence. Eden was like the *Kingdom of Heaven on Earth* for Adam and Eve, and only what was pleasing to the pure and flawless nature of God could dwell there.

...and said, "Assuredly, I say to you, unless you are converted and become as little children, you will by no means enter the kingdom of heaven. – Matthew 18:3

Therefore whoever humbles himself as this little child is the greatest in the kingdom of heaven. – Matthew 18:4

But Jesus said, "Let the little children come to Me, and do not forbid them; for of such is the kingdom of heaven. – Matthew 19:14

But Jesus called them to *Him* and said, "Let the little children come to Me, and do not forbid them; for of such is the kingdom of God. – Luke 18:16

In that hour Jesus rejoiced in the Spirit and said, "I thank You, Father, Lord of heaven and earth, that You have hidden these things from *the* wise and prudent and revealed them to babes. Even so, Father, for so it seemed good in Your sight. – Luke 10:21

Giving full attention to WHAT CHANGED after Adam and Eve did what they did, is the most critical piece of the puzzle in grasping the very concept of sin. This historical event illustrates what sin is in relation to God.

Sin separates us from the will of God. Sin causes us to step outside the will of God. Sin taints, tarnishes and spoils, it turns something clean into something dirty. So, when Lucifer and the angels who followed him (fallen angels » demons) sinned, they were banished from God's presence (Heaven) because only what is clean can be in His presence. Because Lucifer stepped outside of the will of God, he was no longer fit to be in His presence.

So when the woman saw that the tree *was* good for food, that it *was* pleasant to the eyes, and a tree desirable to make *one* wise, she took of its fruit and ate. She also gave to her husband with her, and he ate. Then the eyes of both of them were opened, and they knew that they *were* naked; and they sewed fig leaves together and made themselves coverings.

And they heard the sound of the Lord God walking in the garden in the cool of the day, and Adam and his wife hid themselves from the presence of the Lord God among the trees of the garden.

Then the Lord God called to Adam and said to him, "Where *are* you?"

So he said, "I heard Your voice in the garden, and I was afraid because I was naked; and I hid myself."

And He said, "Who told you that you *were* naked? Have you eaten from the tree of which I commanded you that you should not eat?"

Then the man said, "The woman whom You gave *to be* with me, she gave me of the tree, and I ate."

And the Lord God said to the woman, "What *is* this you have done?"

The woman said, "The serpent deceived me, and I ate." – Genesis 3:6-13

After Lucifer was banished from heaven, he set out to find the next created being to separate from the will of God: humans.

Satan's envy for God's supreme position was demonstrated yet a second time when he challenged God's position of authority and commandment to Adam and Eve: "But of the tree of the knowledge of good and evil you shall not eat, for in the day that you eat of it you shall surely die" (Genesis 2:17).

Only what is pure and untarnished can be considered worthy of living in the presence of God, so Satan sought to stain Adam and Eve's innocence by tempting them with the desires of 'the self'.

He presented to them 'the self' as being equal to or 'like God' and 'the self' as above God: both being expressions of self-exaltation. By disobeying God, they put their desires equal to and above God's commandment. In that moment, they rejected His supremacy and stepped outside His will.

This is pride: exalting | Sin: what separates you from the will of God. | one self, in place of God.

Behold, I *am* against you,
O most haughty one!" says the Lord GOD of hosts;
"For your day has come,
The time *that* I will punish you.
The most proud shall stumble and fall,
And no one will raise him up;
I will kindle a fire in his cities,
And it will devour all around him.
- Jeremiah 50:31-32

"According to Christian teachers, the essential vice, the utmost evil, is Pride. Unchastity, anger, greed, drunkenness, and all that, are mere flea bites in comparison: it was through Pride that the devil became the devil: Pride leads to every other vice: it is the complete anti-God state of mind ... it is Pride which has been the chief cause of misery in every nation and every family since the world began." - C.S. Lewis, *Mere Christianity*

Scripture is clear about how God views pride.

James 4:6, "God resists the proud, But gives grace to the humble."

Matthew 23:12, "And whoever exalts himself will be humbled, and he who humbles himself will be exalted."

1 Samuel 2:3, "Talk no more so very proudly; Let no arrogance come from your mouth, For the Lord is the God of knowledge; And by him actions are weighed."

Romans 12:3, "For I say, through the grace given to me, to everyone who is among you, not to think *of himself* more highly than he ought to think, but to think soberly, as God has dealt to each one a measure of faith."

Proverbs 8:13, "The fear of the Lord *is* to hate evil; Pride and arrogance and the evil way And the perverse mouth I hate."

Isaiah 13:11, "I will punish the world for its evil, And the wicked for their inequity; I will halt the arrogance of the proud, And will lay low the haughtiness of the terrible."

Even though this is not all the scripture on pride, it is a clear indication of how the Lord God feels about pride.

SATAN'S BANISHMENT

Satan was banished from heaven for pride, an action that demonstrates that pride really does lead to destruction. Pride led to the fall of Satan from heaven which in turn led to the fall of man from the garden. And so, as Satan would have it to destroy any goodness that God had created, he tempted Adam and Eve into toying with pride, to consider for them*selves* that they too could "be like God and have their eyes opened to knowing good and evil" (Genesis 3:4), so that they too may fall, just like he did.

By having their eyes opened, the first two humans whom God had created so purely and blamelessly would transform into people with opened / adulterated / mature minds, therefore, ridding them of their childlike characteristics. Being adults they would lose their untainted pure view of the world, as well as their 'childhood' (which is such a precious thing). Without the eyes of a child, they would have an adult perspective on the world, be aware of sinful things and become tempted to desire pleasure from them. Eventually they may question their reliance on God and so develop unbelief, leading to further sin because without an absolute moral code to live by, everything "under the sun" (in the world) (King Solomon: Ecclesiastes 1:9) becomes permissible, leading to even further sin and further separation from God.

I said in my heart, "Come now, I will test you with mirth; therefore enjoy pleasure"; but surely, this also *was* vanity. I said of laughter— "Madness!"; and of mirth, "What does it accomplish?" I searched in my heart *how* to gratify my flesh with wine, while guiding my heart with wisdom, and how to lay hold on folly, till I might see what *was* good for the sons of men to do under heaven all the days of their lives.

I made my works great, I built myself houses, and planted myself vineyards. I made myself gardens and orchards, and I planted all *kinds* of fruit trees in them. I made myself water pools from which to water the growing trees of the grove. I acquired male and female servants, and had servants born in my house. Yes, I had greater possessions of herds and flocks than all who were in Jerusalem before me. I also gathered for myself silver and gold and the special treasures of kings and of the provinces. I acquired male and female singers, the delights of the sons of men, *and* musical instruments of all kinds.

So I became great and excelled more than all who were before me in Jerusalem. Also my wisdom remained with me.

Whatever my eyes desired I did not keep from them. I did not withhold my heart from any pleasure, For my heart rejoiced in all my labor; And this was my reward from all my labor. Then I looked on all the works that my hands had done And on the labor in which I had toiled; And indeed all *was* vanity and grasping for the wind. *There was* no profit under the sun." - Ecclesiastes 2:1-11

Satan led Adam and Eve to exalt their own decision-making ability above what God had instructed them to do. This challenge in the Creator's authority has since travelled from the Garden of Eden through the ages of history and is now growing in contemporary culture where much of society gives credit of *existence* to science, chance, man, technology or evolution. *Very clever indeed.* Satan's aim back then was for man to challenge the truth and severity in the Word of God and thousands and thousands of years later, not much has changed. Unfortunately, many people do not ever consider and see the twist that has taken place and so are blindly led by a false notion of life, which leads to the false notion of death and life after death as well.

Grasping what the exclusion of both Satan, and Adam and Eve from God's Heaven and Garden means, is crucial in understanding how sin excludes us from His presence.

Blessed *are* those who do His commandments, that they may have the right to the tree of life, and may enter through the gates into the city. But outside *are* dogs and sorcerers and sexually immoral and murderers and idolaters, and whoever loves and practices a lie. – Revelations 22:14-15

ALMOST 400 YEARS AGO

Paradise Lost is an impressive wad of literature written by John Milton. The first version of the poem was published in 1667 and consisted of over ten thousand lines of verse, totalling ten books. The second edition followed seven years later and is considered by critics to be Milton's major work confirming his reputation as one of the greatest English poets of his time. The poem is about the Fall of Man: the temptation of Adam and Eve by the fallen angel Satan and their expulsion from the Garden of Eden. The purpose of the poem, as mentioned by Milton himself, is to "justify the ways of God to men", a timely perspective from nearly four hundred years ago.

From Paradise Lost (1667), Book 1 (extracts: lines 1-26; 44-69)

1   Of man's first disobedience, and the fruit
       Of that forbidden tree, whose mortal taste
       Brought death into the world, and all our woe
       With loss of Eden, till one greater Man

5   Restore us, and regain the blissful seat,
Sing heavenly muse, that on the secret top
Of Oreb or of Sinai, didst inspire
That shepherd, who first taught the chosen seed
In the beginning how the heavens and earth

10   Rose out of Chaos: or if Sion Hill
Delight thee more, and Siloa's brook that flowed
Fast by the oracle of God; I thence
Invoke the aid to my adventurous song,
That with no middle flight intends to soar

15   Above the Aonian mount, while it pursues
Things unattempted yet in prose or rhyme.
And chiefly thou, O Spirit, that dost prefer
Before all temples the upright heart and pure,
Instruct me, for thou know'st; thou from the first

20   Wast present, and with mighty wings outspread
Dove-like sat'st brooding on the vast abyss
And mad'st it pregnant: What in me is dark
Illumine, what I slow, raise and support;
That to the height of this great argument
I may assert Eternal Providence, And justify the ways
of God to men.

Satan banished from Heaven
     ...Him the Almighty Power
     Hurled headlong flaming from the ethereal sky
     With hideous ruin and combustion down

30   To bottomless perdition, there to dwell
In adamantine chains and penal fire,
Who durst defy the Omnipotent to arms.

Nine times the space that measures day and night
To mortal men, he with his horrid crew

35   Lay vanquished, rowling in the fiery gulf,
Confounded though immortal: But his doom
Reserved him to more wrath; for now the thought
Both of lost happiness and lasting pain
Torments him; round he throws his baleful eyes

40   That witnessed huge affliction and dismay
Mixed with obdurate pride and steadfast hate:
At once as far as angels' ken and he views
The dismal situation waste and wild,
A dungeon horrible, on all sides round

45   As one great furnace flamed, yet from those flames
No light, but rather darkness visible
Served only to discover sights of woe,
Regions of sorrow, doleful shades, where peace
And rest can never dwell, hope never comes
50   That comes to all; but torture without end

Still urges, and a fiery deluge, fed
With ever-burning sulphur unconsumed.

★★★

The devil became the "ruler of this world" (John 12:31, John 16:11, John 14:30), "the prince of the power of the air" (Ephesians 2:2), and the "god of this world (2 Corinthians 4:4) when he led man, both male and female, to be separated from God through sin. After God passed judgement on Satan, Adam and Eve, "He drove out the man" (Genesis 3:24) from the *heaven on earth* into the rest of the world where they had to then fend for themselves … and still do.

Genesis 3:14-24

So the Lord God said to the serpent:

"Because you have done this,
You are cursed more than all cattle,
And more than every beast of the field;
On your belly you shall go,
And you shall eat dust
All the days of your life.
And I will put enmity
Between you and the woman,
And between your seed and her Seed;
He shall bruise your head,
And you shall bruise His heel."

To the woman He said:

"I will greatly multiply your sorrow and your conception;
In pain you shall bring forth children;
Your desire shall be for your husband,
And he shall rule over you."

Then to Adam He said,

"Because you have heeded the voice of your wife, and have eaten from
the tree of which I commanded you, saying, 'You shall not eat of it':
"Cursed is the ground for your sake;
In toil you shall eat of it
All the days of your life.
Both thorns and thistles it shall bring forth for you,
And you shall eat the herb of the field.
In the sweat of your face you shall eat bread
Till you return to the ground,
For out of it you were taken;
For dust you are,
And to dust you shall return."

And Adam called his wife's name Eve, because she was the mother
of all living.

Also for Adam and his wife the Lord God made tunics of skin, and clothed them.

Then the Lord God said, "Behold, the man has become like one of Us, to know good and evil. And now, lest he put out his hand and take also of the tree of life, and eat, and live forever"— therefore the Lord God sent him out of the garden of Eden to till the ground from which he was taken. So He drove out the man; and He placed cherubim at the east of the garden of Eden, and a flaming sword which turned every way, to guard the way to the tree of life.

Since Eve was "the mother of all living" (Genesis 3:20), her sin is carried through from generation to generation and that is why every human being is born as a sinner. The first sin caused everyone to be born a sinner, with the potential to sin.

We are genetically inclined to be sinful and so the only way to be acquitted of this inherent gene of sin that each and every one of us carries,

> … is to be reborn.

Ok, wow! So, there's a way out – what good news to me.

Not in the flesh, because that is physically impossible, but in the spirit, which is possible.

There was a man of the Pharisees named Nicodemus, a ruler of the Jews. [2] This man came to Jesus by night and said to Him, "Rabbi, we know that You are a teacher come from God; for no one can do these signs that You do unless God is with him."

Jesus answered and said to him, "Most assuredly, I say to you, unless one is born [a]again, he cannot see the kingdom of God."

Nicodemus said to Him, "How can a man be born when he is old? Can he enter a second time into his mother's womb and be born?"

Jesus answered, "Most assuredly, I say to you, unless one is born of water and the Spirit, he cannot enter the kingdom of God. That which is born of the flesh is flesh, and that which is born of the Spirit is spirit. Do not marvel that I said to you, 'You must be born again.' The wind blows where it wishes, and you hear the sound of it, but cannot tell where it comes from and where it goes. So is everyone who is born of the Spirit." – John 3:1-7

What do I do now, now that I know I am a sinner and need to be reborn?

PART
THREE

At first the truth hurts ... and then it shall set you free

Why does the truth hurt?

Why does the truth hurt so much?

I'm yet to come across anyone who has ever been faced with an awkward fact or sore truth about themselves and enjoys hearing it. Which is why *the truth* is so hard to accept and is most often avoided or covered up. It's easier to simply sweep it away where it can't be dealt with.

The truth is hard to hear because it gets to the *crux of the matter,*

Crux:
the most important or serious part of
a matter, problem, or argument.

---

and hits a nerve that only the receiver knows has been affected. Only the receiver would know what being said is actually true. The message could hurt so badly that one may even resent the messenger for sharing it. Like when somebody tells you directly that you're arrogant or weak, judgemental or lazy, it really hurts. But when its true, only you will know. It is in these moments where the hard truth sinks in and cuts straight to your marrow. It is in these moments where we have the opportunity to grow from these morsels of truths about oneself, turning it into a teaching moment. Even though the words were hurtful, they were helpful.

'IGNORANCE IS BLISS' IS SHORT LIVED

Ever hear the phrase, "Ignorance is bliss"? After seeing it on a bumper sticker, I used it many times afterwards to dodge impending consequences. But as catchy as it is, unfortunately this concept has a lifespan with an expiry date. After a while, and after one too many times of referencing it, one realises there is no real sincere longevity in it. It is absolutely unsustainable for any great length of time because at some point in life, one must *face up* to the truth about oneself, about reality, about life, and about death - leaving being 'ignorant' hopelessly null and void. One cannot go on for too long holding onto 'blissful ignorance', it'll get you into serious trouble and cannot save you.

There are many people who have let their *guard down*, so have fallen into the growing popular trap that condones or even endorses this "ignorance is bliss" pattern of thinking with regards to the serious questions in life. Choosing not to think about life in its entirety, doesn't change the fact that the serious life questions still remain and still need answering. At some point, every single person ought to consider "Who am I?", "What is my purpose?", or at the very least "Why am I even here?"

Which brings me to another common phrase.

"The truth shall set you free".

When I first heard this phrase, I thought it sounded cool and left it there but it is only until my first-hand experience with it, did I realise how magnificently colossal and far-reaching it really is.

How will the truth set you free?

Let's take it one step further

What will it free you from?

In tackling the answers to the previous two big questions in bold – "How will the truth set you free?" and "What will it free you from?" I will do so within a general mainstream capacity before being specific and sharing my first-hand experience.

DOWN THE RABBIT HOLE

A film entitled *The Matrix (1999)* illustrates the answers to these two questions in a perfectly visual way. If you haven't seen the film, please do so because the cinematography provides a hardcore visual depiction on **truth** and **blindness** and how serious these aspects really are.

(In no way am I endorsing the personal philosophy of the author/s of the film, I am simply referring to it because of its excellent illustrative ability in demonstrating the sobering reality that each one of us faces. Truth v blindness)

Depicted in a dystopian future in the year 2199, *The Matrix (1999)* is a science fiction action film in which the reality that is perceived and lived out by humans is actually a fake world called 'the matrix' that has been produced by machines with artificial intelligence. The main character Thomas Anderson with the alias 'Neo' (Keanu Reeves) sets out to uncover what this matrix is. In one of the initial scenes, Neo (Keanu Reeves) meets up with Morpheus (Laurence Fishburne) who has been searching for Neo his entire life because he believes that Neo is the only man who can overcome this machine produced matrix.

In this meeting between Morpheus and Neo, they have a conversation that sets into motion a whirlwind of discovering that the matrix really does exist and that he has been right all along about the control of the machines. The concept of this scene, where Morpheus presents to Neo an option between a red and blue pill, each with differing consequences, is a very thought-provoking scenario because it mirrors the decisions we humans make. Do we remain stagnated in comfort, and continue living and believing whatever we want to believe? Or do we choose to hear the truth – the real truth – no matter how hard it will be to absorb? The outcome of the choice that Neo makes ignites a chain of events that is so mind-blowingly accurate because he chooses the red pill: he chooses to hear the truth.

The reason for referencing this film as a springboard for my explanation on *discovering the truth* is because what happened to Neo in the Matrix,

… happened to me.

FIRST HAND EXPERIENCE: choosing the red pill

In May 2016, during the final exam period in the last semester of my Bachelor of Arts degree, I developed the most intense hunger for Scripture I had ever experienced in my life. I just couldn't get enough of the Word of God; it had come alive to me. The funniest thing is, is that it was the Old Testament that had penetrated me so deeply and not the New as would be expected. When I discovered the rich history of the Old Testament and started learning about Hebrew culture, the Hebrew language and Jewish food, the Bible transformed from a very important book to an accurate account of historical and supernatural truth that transformed my very sight. When I realised that the Bible is a recording of what took place thousands of years ago in the Middle East between God and men and not just a compilation of stories for good morality, bedtime reading and Sunday school classes, my entire world changed. *This was real.*

It is this falling in adoration for the Old Testament and the history before Christ on earth, that finally confirmed that my Christian faith was real, because it is real. I had now developed genuine belief. The history of the Jewish nation and how they wrestled with God in a geographical region that still exists today with archaeological proof that supports everything written in the Bible, completely captivated me. I had finally reached a point where I knew for certain, without any doubt, what I believed in. *It was all real.*

I then began reading areas of Scripture I had NEVER EVER before encountered in all my years of church going and it simply blew me away. I started gathering books and audio sermons by various teachers and even attended my first ever Jewish Passover Festival at a local church. Well, that was it, I was convinced. Diving into history is generally fascinating, but swimming through God's history or 'HIStory' with the human race is phenomenal. There is absolutely no way one can think the same as you did before after being soaked in its splendour.

To come to terms with the Old Testament requires a massive mind shift because what happened in those thirty-nine books is hard, its raw, its unthinkable, its unfathomable, it's tough to swallow, it's frightening, and even shocking at times. The collection of books that constitute the Bible are unlike any other piece of literature because there is no sugar coating available for easy digestion. It's not designed to please or to impress, it was written to record what happened and what will happen. It is real.

There are parts to the Old Testament that can be demanding to read with many stretched out bits, i.e., the pages and pages of laws, commandments and on-going genealogies with much 'begetting' to read through. But what seems as being tedious to read, emerges a deep richness like no other. The fullness of this library of books is unparalleled and when one starts unpacking each book, the purpose behind these so called tedious laws, commandments and on-going genealogies is revealed, generating a tapestry that makes perfect sense when viewed as one body of work. "The law of the Lord is perfect, converting the soul" (Psalm 19:7).

How can a young man cleanse his way?
By taking heed according to Your word.
With my whole heart I have sought You;
Oh, let me not wander from Your commandments!
Your word I have hidden in my heart,
That I might not sin against You.
Blessed *are* You, O LORD!
Teach me Your statutes.
With my lips I have declared
All the judgments of Your mouth.
I have rejoiced in the way of Your testimonies,
As *much as* in all riches.
I will meditate on Your precepts,
And contemplate Your ways.
I will delight myself in Your statutes;
I will not forget Your word. – Psalm 119: 9 – 16

During this period of hunger, I spent a lot of time reading the Bible, fasting and seeking prayer. I just couldn't get enough of what I was discovering. There was a slight problem though, I was in the middle of my final exams and so I asked God to keep me eager until just after my exams so that I could concentrate on my studies and at the very least pass everything. Miraculously, the Lord carried me through each and every subject, even with my preoccupied mind, my results were pleasingly high upon completion.

And you will seek Me and find *Me,* when you search for Me with all your heart. - Jeremiah 29:13

FIRST HAND EXPERIENCE: swallowing the red pill

"Ask, and it will be given to you; seek, and you will find; knock, and it will be opened to you" (Matthew 7:7-11), so that is what I did.

I requested to meet up with two ladies from a neighbouring church to hear about their experiences in a local ministry. They told me of the wondrous things they had experienced and seen, and then asked me whether they could pray for me. Thoughtfully I said, "Yes please. I would like for God to use and touch my mouth, so let us pray for that because that is what I am yearning for."

I had been seeking for God to reveal something special and revelatory from Him to me. For me to speak correctly and truthfully about Him, and for Him to use my lips. *This is what I desired!*

Let the words of my mouth and the meditation of my heart be acceptable in Your sight, O Lord, my strength and my Redeemer. - Psalm 19:14

After the meet up at the house, we said our goodbyes and went our separate ways. Me still yearning for the Lord to reveal something from Him to me.

But then,

about two weeks later

… something ineffable happened.

Ineffable: too great or extreme to be expressed or
described in words; or, not to be uttered.

I was smacked over the head.

It felt as if I had been smacked over the head to the floor in the lounge of the house where I had been prayed for.

I also saw myself sprawled out face down on my stomach in the lounge of the house where I had been prayed for.

… knocked with the Spirit of truth.

It happened exactly like that.

I felt hit over the head and saw myself prostrated on the floor.

But when the Helper comes, whom I shall send to you from the Father, the Spirit of truth who proceeds from the Father, He will testify of me. And you also will bear witness, because you have been with Me from the beginning. - John 15: 26

The extraordinary thing is, is that I'd never been back to the house. So how could I have been knocked to the floor of the lounge. And, I had never actually been hit.

Therefore, what followed must have happened with my spirit.

There are diversities of gifts, but the same Spirit. There are differences of ministries, but the same Lord. And there are diversities of activities, but it is the same God who works all in all. But the manifestation of the Spirit is given to each one for the profit *of all:* for to one is given the word of wisdom through the Spirit, to another the word of knowledge through the same Spirit, to another faith by the same Spirit, to another gifts of healings by the same Spirit, to another the working of miracles, to another prophecy, to another discerning of spirits, to another *different* kinds of tongues, to another the interpretation of tongues. But one and the same Spirit works all these things, distributing to each one individually as He wills. - 1 Corinthians 12: 1-11

And then I was HIT with the following words ...

"JESUS IS TRUTH"

"JESUS IS TRUTH"

"JESUS IS TRUTH"

I still have many things to say to you, but you cannot bear *them* now. However, when He, the Spirit of truth, has come, He will guide you into all truth; for He will not speak on His own *authority*, but whatever He hears He will speak; and He will tell you things to come. He will glorify Me, for He will take of what is Mine and declare *it* to you. All things that the Father has are Mine. Therefore I said that He will take of Mine and declare *it* to you. – *Jesus*, John 16:12-15

HEARING *WORDS* FROM GOD

When I refer to *words*, I am referring to a whole-body communication where the words not only enter your ears (like when speaking to another person) they also enter your mind, your skin, your tongue, your lips, your heart, your entire being. The Word that God gives you through His Spirit, is His language - it is a whole-body language. You not only hear the Words He communicates to you but you feel them, you sense them, you are filled with them. You drink them in like *living water*.

For the word of God *is* living and powerful, and sharper than any two-edged sword, piercing even to the division of soul and spirit, and of joints and marrow, and is a discerner of the thoughts and intents of the heart. – Hebrews 4:12

Language is a gift from God and communication from Him is multi-dimensional. When He speaks to His children, they recognise His voice.

So, in this vivid moment where the words "JESUS IS TRUTH" filled me.

Another thing happened,

beyond surreal

... my eyes were opened.

Amazing Grace, How sweet the sound
That saved a wretch like me
I once was lost, but now am found
T'was blind but now I see.
Lyrics to Amazing Grace (1772) John Newton

My eyes were opened in such a way that I not only saw with new eyes but felt and realised with a new heart and new mind. The knowledge and awareness I received in that moment and in the weeks that followed was transformational. It was life-changing. The Words – JESUS IS TRUTH - were multi-dimensional, almost outer-planetary, and they changed me completely.

When my eyes opened, two aspects were revealed to me:

1.   The truth about the world we live in (at first the truth hurts)
2.   Who Jesus really is (and then it shall set you free)

AT FIRST THE TRUTH HURTS, AND THEN YOU'LL BE THANKFUL FOR IT

"Excuse me Candace, you have a piece of spinach stuck in between your teeth." As confronting as that is for anyone receiving such embarrassing news, it's rather helpful. I'd much prefer someone telling me this piece of truth than ignoring it all the while through our conversation pretending that the big wet greenish leaf never existed.

What's even worse is when a friend or someone you know doesn't tell you and allows you to move on to another conversation with someone else even though the spinach is still flapping about. I definitely think it's better to be embarrassed for those few seconds by someone at the start than to realise afterwards that the person didn't care enough to tell you. I'd rather the truth hurt for those few seconds from someone you know than for much longer and for a much harsher period.

One of the most hurtful things you can do to someone, is not tell them the truth.

It might seem silly to use the example of spinach stuck in your teeth when discussing the heavily serious topic of the truth, but the point being made is the same. It is helpful when someone points out that you have "spinach in your teeth", a remark that only hurts for those embarrassing few seconds, but can save you further future embarrassment. It is also helpful (and compellingly more so) pointing out that "without Jesus you will be separated from God for all eternity, without Jesus you are outside the will of God, repent and turn away from your sins because your sin is what separates you from God, if you die tomorrow without the atoning grace of Christ you die in your sin and die separated from God." This is *the truth*, and it will hurt you the first time you hear it if you don't already know it. It will hurt because it's shocking, it's raw, it's real and life-altering. This truth will challenge you to assess on which side of the city gates you stand. Are you standing in the midst of truth or are you standing outside the city in darkness? Have you come to realise this truth? Do you understand it? Without the atoning blood of Jesus, your sins remain with you when you die causing you to be separated from God for all eternity. Only those who believe in the work of the Lamb of God can be saved.

Ask yourself, why did Jesus come to earth? Why did God send Him? When I first realised the answers to these questions, I was awestruck, totally in awe of Jesus Christ. I very soon understood how thankful I must be for Him. He made a way! *Thank you, Jesus.*

Just imagine not telling someone the truth about Jesus and that only through Him can anyone be with God and live in Heaven. Think about how that omission of the truth would hurt, it will hurt for all eternity. This is why sharing *the Truth* is so urgently important.

Brethren, if anyone among you wanders from the truth, and someone turns him back, let him know that he who turns a sinner from the error of his way will save a soul from death and cover a multitude of sins. – James 5:19-20

This above passage from the book of James is what drives me to share what God has revealed to me. In fact, I imagine shouting it from the rooftops. The truth must be shared, especially the one that impacts our eternity.

Therefore do not fear them. For there is nothing covered that will not be revealed, and hidden that will not be known. Whatever I tell you in the dark, speak in the light; and what you hear in the ear, preach on the housetops. And do not fear those who kill the body but cannot kill the soul. But rather fear Him who is able to destroy both soul and body in hell. – Matthew 10: 26-28

The truth hurts because it is uncomfortable and presents a challenge. Its uncomfortable because you're confronted about something you have a fault with or because it conflicts with your pre-existing attitude. The truth can be even more difficult to hear when it confronts with a belief strongly engrained in you. This is especially true when your pre-existing attitude is also already hostile, or even comfortably nonchalant.

Once one hears the truth, one can either choose to accept it or deny it. It's like accepting that you didn't brush your teeth properly or that you failed to look in the mirror before you left home and now you have a piece of spinach flapping about your mouth, one can either grow from the advice or notification, or deny it and continue meeting and greeting people with an offensive slice of vegetable obscuring their vision. Both reactions have consequences.

The implication of denying the truth about yourself or never facing up to anything that presents a challenge in accepting the truth about yourself, you will unfortunately take yourself down a path towards stagnation and then inevitably failure. If one does not change, one does not grow. And like anything else on the planet that does not grow and is not nurtured, it becomes ineffective, purposeless and eventually dies. If we take the analogy one step further and say that while denying the truth about oneself, we eventually cease to move and grow, the same is true for denying the truth to life itself, we shall cease to grow and like the plant that is not watered, you shall also wither and die.

Change inspires growth.

A human death is not only physical but can also be emotional and spiritual too, so when one ceases to grow emotionally, this is also considered to be a *deathlike state of existence*. Without emotion, you are incapable of showing love, having compassion and feeling empathy, leaving you in basic survival mode and simply tending to your bodily needs in order to continue breathing. This is hardly being alive. The same goes for ceasing to nurture our spiritual and emotional growth, we are left cut off from our true created nature.

Therefore, once we have learnt the truth, is it not paramount for our own sakes to make the choice between accepting it in order to grow or denying it which leaves you blinded.

Just like in the scene in *The Matrix* (1999) where Neo has been unplugged from the device that connects him to the machine world, and now finally sees the reality of the world he has been living in his whole life with his own eyes, he realises how sickening and appalling it truly is. He sees the empty depravity of his previous existence. What he once identified with as being 'all that he knew' and 'his truth', stares at him face-to-face, and now seems deathlike. Once Neo wakes up, Morpheus asks him, "If you could go back, would you really want to?".

This is exactly where I find myself as a result of what God showed me. There is no way I could return to the identity I once thought was 'real'. Realising the empty depravity of the place I once *lived in*, I am thankful that my eyes were opened and now I see *the Truth*.

Below are the two aspects that became really crystal clear to me during this spiritual awakening:

REVEALING OF ASPECT 1

1. The truth about the world we live in
    a. Satan's attack
    b. Starting to see
    c. Lifting the veil
    d. Discernment
    e. Eventually seeing clearly through frosted glass

a. SATAN'S ATTACK

Satan's main aim is to keep you from seeing *the truth*. He will even present you with half a truth that seems safe, comfortable, even pleasant on the surface. Perhaps this version even has decent intentions but really doesn't because it's not in line with the *Image of God*. Satan was the first rebellious creature, followed by the other fallen angels (demons) whose desire is for all men and women to be separated from God in various ways. Just as Satan separated himself from God with his sin, he too caused the first man and woman to be separated from God with their sin and desires to separate men and women today with their sin.

Satan's ultimate desire is for humans to die
being separated from God.
Satan's ultimate desire is for humans to die
with their sin.
Satan's ultimate desire is for humans to die
as unrepented sinners.

All of the above leaves humans separated from God.

In the moment where Satan interacted with Adam and Eve in the garden, he undertook to taint the *Image of God,* and the *Image of God* is G(g)ood. When God was creating in the beginning, He said that what He saw "was good" (Genesis 1:10). Satan came to attack this G(g)ood(ness) and taint it with (d)evil.

Firstly: he approached and tempted Eve before Adam because within the *Image of God,* man was created before the woman which established Adam as the head of the family (Genesis 2:18-25). By putting Eve's voice above Adam's, Satan reversed (put the wrong way up) the matrimonial structure that God had designed and placed second (second created woman) above first (first created man).

Anything Satan can do to overturn or stain the *Image of God* will suit his desire for leading people away from God and seeing the truth in *God's Image.* After Adam and Eve's disobedience, God immediately called for Adam (first) because God had *commanded* Adam even before

Eve was created so Adam had always been fully aware of what God had commanded, which made him responsible for his actions regardless of how he came to disobey God. Adam was also established as the head.

Genesis 3:17

"Because you have heeded the voice of your wife, and have eaten from the tree of which I commanded you, saying, 'You shall not eat of it':

"Cursed is the ground for your sake;
In toil you shall eat of it
All the days of your life.
Both thorns and thistles it shall bring forth for you,
And you shall eat the herb of the field.
In the sweat of your face you shall eat bread
Till you return to the ground,
For out of it you were taken;
For dust you are,
And to dust you shall return."

Besides passing judgment on Adam for not obeying His commandment, God also demonstrated with Adam's judgment how fundamental hierarchy and structure, design and order is in the Kingdom of Heaven and that God's vision for the world was always the ultimate G(g)ood and the best way to have it.

Satan will attack *God's design* anywhere he can. Even today, in the 21ˢᵗ century, this attack is blatant to those who are seeking *the Truth* or the *Image of God* in the world around us.

One-way Satan attacks the *Image of God* is by offending His written Word. One tactic is to offend the first book of the Bible, Genesis, especially the first three chapters where God reveals how He created the natural world: the universe, earth and humans. The Bible deals with the beginning of Creation and also how the first man and woman were created in *His Image* in these first three chapters but Satan attacks this account by seducing an individual with alternative theories intended to cause doubt in the way God said that it happened. These theories range from evolutionary ones to the concept of a big bang, with the list going on I am sure. Ultimately, Satan's goal is to distort the truth by removing God from it all, resulting in-a-world-without-God-state of mind.

Unfortunately for these readers and conveniently for Satan, once you doubt the authority of Genesis, the other 65 books of the Bible become irrelevant to that person and so the rest of the truth gets ignored. By separating yourself from these other books of the Bible, you are essentially choosing the blue pill which allows you to continue "living as you did before and believing whatever you want to believe" instead of choosing the red pill that takes you on a journey to facing the truth.

b. STARTING TO SEE

During the few months where God was revealing the first portion of this revelation (this chapter) to me it was then that I started compiling this book. The writing began almost as soon as my exams were completed. As I said before, it was not until I had become *the messenger* God wanted me to be could I ever have been able to produce one-hundred-and-ninety or so pages. There is unequivocally no way.

It was during the time from about May to July of 2016 where I soared into a spiritual high because of what I was learning and realising. It was like 'seeing' for the first time. These two to three months were incredible and felt as if I was walking on clouds. Even though the clarification I received was out-of-this-world, I personally don't think God intends one to remain on this cloud of awe for an extended period of time because we're also only human and need to continue living 'earthed'. I don't think I could have handled anymore spiritual height because it was too awesome. At some point one must come back down to earth to continue "fight(ing) the good fight of faith" (1 Timothy 6:12) and so I was only given about two to three months of this overwhelming experience.

The Matrix (1999) once again illustrates this aspect of my experience again. After Neo has been shot at repeatedly by the opposing agents, they presume him to be dead and begin walking away down the passage to leave the building. Once Neo comes to and stands up, the camera frames him looking at the agents walking away but then as the angle changes to frame what he is looking at, the viewer sees the agents as Neo sees them now. Not in the usual way as the viewer has seen them throughout the film, but now as mere code and strings of programming. He therefore sees them for what they truly are, how they are constructed and right through them.

Over the course of two to three months, I began seeing the social construct – the artificiality - the lie – the veil – the half-truth – the depravity – the pride of the world around us. I saw it for what it is, I saw it clearly (just in the way Neo did). It was as if frosted glass had been replaced with a clear translucent one and I saw straight through the smokescreen of *the pride of life*. I saw how empty the world was, how meaningless human ambition and the drive for progress really is. I saw how pointless it is when separated from *Truth* and how this produced world we live in, is not *the truth*. I saw the hand of Satan in how he has led humans to artificially produce an existence in which we think to be real, but really isn't. It's actually just a false reality, a biding of time in which many obtain their definitions from, which in turn establishes their false identity.

Certain aspects of daily life also changed, in particular colours. They became illuminated and shone with a brighter hue than usual. It was as if I was seeing with new eyes and became more aware of creation around me. I felt as though I was now aware of something that was so blatantly obvious to me because my eyes were now open. I couldn't understand how other people were so unaware of their blindness, blissfully ignorant and 'unwanting of true sight'.

This can seem far-fetched but one must remember that there is a mystery to the workings of God that is "hidden in God" (Ephesians 3:9). Ephesians 3:3 speaks of "the mystery made known to me by revelation", Ephesians 1:9 refers to the "mystery of His will" and Colossians 1:26-27 reads, "the mystery which has been hidden from ages and from generations, but now has been revealed to His saints. To them God willed to make known what are the riches of the glory of this mystery among the Gentiles: which is Christ in you, the hope of glory".

c. LIFTING THE VEIL

The Bible speaks of an *unveiling*. Just like the veil of a bride that covers her face as she stands before the altar with her soon-to-be-husband while hiding her true identity from him. Behind the hidden cloth, he anticipates her true nature to be revealed. Once her veil is lifted, both parties are then able to see each other clearly. In the same way as her eyes and face were once covered and then after were freed to behold her husband in true reality and vice versa, the same is true when God removes the veil from our eyes in order for us to see Him for who He is and for Him to see us in a new way. We are exposed to Him and He to us (at His choosing) in a meeting that is *mysteriously* sacred and intimate: sometimes too special to even share with others because in that private moment you were mirrored – and so reflected the glory of the Lord because you stared right *into the eyes* of the Image Creator. "But we all, with unveiled face, beholding as in a mirror the glory of the Lord, are being transformed into the same image from glory to glory, just as by the Spirit of the Lord" (2 Corinthians 3:8).

A very sad but true story comes to mind as I write this section but I must share it in order to expand on the greater symbolism of mirroring. A political prisoner in Eastern Europe was imprisoned for roughly forty years for political crimes he committed in his twenties. With having spent most of his life inside prison, when released he was asked whether there was anything he would like. He replied, "I would like a mirror, because I have not seen my face in forty years." When handed the mirror, he just sobbed.

I can't even begin to imagine the suffering and isolation that this man must have experienced inside those prison walls. With never having had access to many people, let alone not seeing his very own reflection, he must have endured such agony.

What emerges for me as the most profound element of this story is the way in which it parallels with people who don't know God. Not being in relation to God means they have never looked into the face of the *Image Creator*, therefore never seeing their true reflection. They do not reflect the face of the *Image Creator* and so are not *Image Bearers*. Without reflecting off and looking into their true nature, they are essentially living their lives in the same isolation. We were all created in the *Image of God* but when one doesn't see that, you really don't see your true identity. Our very created nature is reflective of who God is and the two ought to mirror one another. How terrible it is for those who will die and have never uncovered their faces to see their real reflection, revealing who they truly are.

Only after seeking the Lord will you then discover your true identity because His very nature reflects onto you.

The symbolism of the veil runs from the Old to the New Testament and is important in noting how God desires to relate to us and what Jesus did in order for this to happen. In the Old Testament the veil was used to divide the sections of the tabernacle into sections of holiness.

Exodus 26:31-35

"You shall make a veil woven of blue, purple, and scarlet thread, and fine woven linen. It shall be woven with an artistic design of cherubim. You shall hang it upon the four pillars of acacia wood overlaid with gold. Their hooks shall be gold, upon four sockets of silver. And you shall hang the veil from the clasps. Then you shall bring the ark of the Testimony in there, behind the veil. The veil shall be a divider for you between the holy place and the Most Holy. You shall put the mercy seat upon the ark of the Testimony in the Most Holy. You shall set the table outside the veil, and the lampstand across from the table on the side of the tabernacle toward the south; and you shall put the table on the north side."

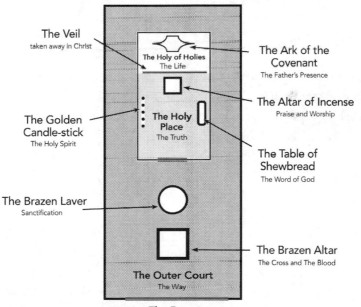

The veil separated the holy place from the Most Holy (Exodus 26:33), as well as the Ark of the Covenant from view. Only the high priest entered the Holy of Holies, once a year on Yom Kippur or Day of Atonement (Leviticus 16).

At the moment Jesus was crucified (New Testament), "Jesus cried out, and breathed His last" (Mark 15:37), "the veil of the temple was torn in two from top to bottom" (Mark 15:38). Jesus' death immediately changed the way we relate to God because Jesus broke that separation between us and God through His atoning sacrifice. He did this so that we could be reconciled to our Heavenly Father. Only what is *clean and without blemish* can be in the presence of the Father, so with the blood that Jesus shed, we have a means to do that. When the veil of the law in the Old Testament tore, it indicated how we are now able to speak directly to God through the Grace of Christ. We don't need to go through any human priest or human pastor to reach God, we go directly to God through the work of Christ on the Cross. Only through Jesus can we reach God.

Thank you, Jesus.

This is what the unveiling does, it allows us to see and be seen directly by our *Image Creator*: God. It is this unveiling that opens our eyes. It is this unveiling that removes our blindness to *the Truth* – and Jesus is *the Truth*.

d. DISCERNMENT

The word *discern* and its extensions are translated from the Greek word *anakrino* in the New Testament. It means *to separate out by diligent searching, to distinguish, to examine*. Discernment is the capacity to properly differentiate or make determinations. The Word of God itself is said to discern the thoughts and intentions of one's heart, "For the word of God is living and powerful, and sharper than any two-edged sword, piercing even to the division of soul and spirit, and of joints and marrow, and is a discerner of the thoughts and intents of the heart" (Hebrews 4:12). A discerning mind reveals wisdom and awareness that goes beyond what is naturally heard and seen. To the human mind without the Spirit, the things of God are "foolishness". The Spirit then gives us spiritual discernment. "But the natural man does not receive the things of the Spirit of God, for they are foolishness to him; nor can he know them, because they are spiritually discerned" (1 Corinthians 2:14).

During my period of spiritual clarification, my level of discernment was at a peak. I could see behind the smokescreen that blinds us normally to the lie. My eyes had been opened and I started noticing the difference between an obvious lie and what was painted as truth but really wasn't true at all. Surely the blatantly obvious lies are pushed aside but when you are left with the ones that appeal to the overall common good, that's when discernment gets tricky.

Something may also appear to be truthful because it is a half-truth, which is deceiving because it has elements of truth to it. All the devil has to do is to present something that appears to be correct, naturally catching a lot of people off guard, but under the surface of it, it has evil motives. Satan is the "angel of light" after all, "And no wonder! Satan transforms himself into an angel of light" (2 Corinthians 11:14). It is discernment that helps us determine what is from God and what is not.

e. EVENTUALLY SEEING CLEARLY THROUGH FROSTED GLASS: WHAT I SAW INTO

And do not be conformed to this world, but be transformed by the renewing of your mind, that you may prove what *is* that good and acceptable and perfect will of God. - Romans 12:2

A lot of what I saw into was actually media based, I think because it is the most accessible means of relaying a message, transmitting an agenda and influencing worldviews. Most media platforms are entertaining so it's an especially easy conduit of communication. In our hedonistic, pleasure seeking societies, anything that is entertaining is appealing. So, what better way to send a subliminal message or agenda through than when you are least expecting it. Our guards are down when we are being entertained, so we tend to let a lot of things slide past our conscience because we're simply relaxing on the couch.

During this period where my eyes were opened, I saw deeper into the constructs of this world and got a real sense of its purpose or agenda. I saw further into the various media platforms and how easily 'the world's anti-Truth and Truth-opposing-agenda' is given a voice through which to speak to its many listeners.

Communication platforms like television advertisements, mainstream music, mainstream film, mainstream radio, social media, mainstream news and even large-scale award ceremonies became afflicting to watch during this peak of spiritual clarity because of how it contradicted to the *truth radar* growing inside of me.

The Spirit of truth, whom the world cannot receive, because it neither sees Him nor knows Him; but you know Him, for He dwells with you and will be in you. - John 14:17.

A 360 ABOUT FILM

The funniest thing after your mind is renewed, is the moment you notice for yourself the contrast in your own thinking when compared to before. 'Doing a 360' is the place you arrive at when you've done a full circle moment in your own thinking. It is the place where you stare in the face of the same challenges and obstacles that you have faced before, in an earlier stage of your life, with only the underdeveloped and limited understanding of the young person you once were. But now, years later, you face the same challenges with maturity and more life tools in your bag. With these tools of experience and wisdom, you're then able to resolve these same challenges with developed problem-solving techniques and hindsight. The beauty of this full circle life movement is that you can now avoid making the same mistakes of the past as well as making better choices because of a renewed mind.

Film in particular is an example where I have clearly *done a 360*, because trying to watch the same film now as I did before my mind was renewed, often leaves me speechless when I consider how I digested such garbage in the first place. *How on earth could I have ever thought this was appealing or even interesting?*

I also now see very clearly how obvious the underhanded message is in some of the mainstream films I used to be able to watch, as well as how terribly twisted some of them can be. It couldn't be more apparent how these messages are a complete lie and totally oppose *the Truth,* as they are produced by the father of lies (John 8:44).

You are of *your* father the devil, and the desires of your father you want to do. He was a murderer from the beginning, and does not stand in the truth, because there is no truth in him. When he speaks a lie, he speaks from his own *resources,* for he is a liar and the father of it. - John 8:44

Any art form is simply a message produced by a messenger, being relayed from the artist to the receiver. I would have battled to see it before but now I am able to see the message quite blatantly and can't even sit through five minutes of the type of *junk* I could previously consume. With the prospect of enjoying the humour and a morsel of romance, the genre of film most easily affected and easily ingested by subliminal or even blatant messaging, would be comedies and romantic comedies. Humour is funny that way – it has a way of giving something pernicious, indirect permission to slip through the cracks of caution.

Pernicious: having a harmful effect, especially in a gradual or subtle way. Late Middle English: from Latin pernicious 'destructive', from pernicies 'ruin', based on nex, nec- 'death'.

A CURIOUS PORTAL

Etymology is the study of the origin of words, an area of Linguistics I find fascinating because this is where definitions are born. Definitions give language structure because they give words meaning, and with meaning comes communication. When you begin exploring definitions, it is the history of the word through the ages as well as its core meaning that provides the best perspective when determining what the word really implies today and why it has been used in a given situation. It is the root and the essence from where it comes that provides context and clarity for the decipherer (a person who converts text or code into normal language).

When we look at definitions, including the root of it as well as its historical changes, we gain additional perspective on why that word has been used today. With reference to my above revelation on media, I'll provide one definition below to tickle your thinking hats with. I hope this definition provides meaning to the message.

Device:

1. a thing made or adapted for a particular purpose, especially a piece of mechanical or electronic equipment.

2. a plan, method, or trick with a particular aim.

Middle English: from Old French devis, based on Latin divis- 'divided', from the verb dividere. The original sense was 'desire or intention', found now only in leave someone to their own devices (which has become associated with device (sense 2)).

LEARNING FROM WHAT KING
SOLOMON EXPERIENCED

I could go on endlessly about this worldview or the fabricated stage around us, all of it constructed to distract and draw our attention from the real truth. Even just reminiscing on what I saw into, stirs feelings of resentment towards the world, but I must share it because it's part of the message and I want the message to be real, truthful and purposeful. The *worldly veil* is thick and separates people without difficulty from their true and designed identity because humans are so easily led astray with the here-and-now and what they see right in front of them. Most of us go about blindly chasing a conjured dream of success and lifestyle, as if that is the sole purpose of our lives, but it isn't. This blind struggle of a fabricated dream is part of the lie, which can only lead us falsely - because it's a distraction. The veil is so thick for some that they live each day without ever realising the truth in what Jesus says, "Do not love the world or the things in the world. If anyone loves the world, the love of the Father is not in him. For all that is in the world—the lust of the flesh, the lust of the eyes, and the pride of life—is not of the Father but is of the world. And the world is passing away, and the lust of it; but he who does the will of God abides forever" (1 John 2:15-17).

After seeing the world around me after having the *veil* lifted, I can sincerely say I felt and still begrudgingly feel the same disheartening gloom that king Solomon writes about in the book of Ecclesiastes. On some days, I think it more depends on where I am and what I am doing, I sense a strong gloom with the unapologetic carnality and depravity of society, almost to the point of, "What is the point of living amidst this lie? If only these people knew how false it all was. How do they go about their day without a thought about anything other than these constant temporary desires?" Then God renews me and restores my strength and gives me vigour to continue fighting the faith and shining my light because we are here on earth to fulfil His purpose for our lives and to glorify Him – and that is exciting!

King Solomon reigned between 970 – 931 BC and during his rule he had great riches, women, education, power, wisdom, grandeur, success, achievement and any entertainment and pleasure he could summon, but still felt empty and unsatisfied, even to the point of questioning the purpose of life after acquiring it all. What was the point of collecting and gathering all this earthly wealth and enjoyment if it left him feeling discouraged and unfulfilled, he wondered? The act of seeking one stimulant after the next had become unsatisfying and meaningless. None of it gave him true and long-lasting fulfilment and peace. More wealth and more women, more riches and more entertainment would not heal the emptiness he experienced.

In Ecclesiastes 1:1-8, King Solomon uses the word *vanity* which in that time period of usage possessed the added element of 'emptiness' to its meaning, when today *vanity* merely refers to the pride over one's physical appearance. (This is another example as to why we must look at the history and root of a word when seeking clarity about the full meaning of a word because it provides us with the full message and proper communication).

Ecclesiastes 1: 1-8

"The words of the Preacher, the son of David, king in Jerusalem.
"Vanity of vanities," says the Preacher;
"Vanity of vanities, all is vanity."

What profit has a man from all his labour
In which he toils under the sun?
One generation passes away, and another generation comes;
But the earth abides forever.

The sun also rises, and the sun goes down,
And hastens to the place where it arose.
The wind goes toward the south,
And turns around to the north;
The wind whirls about continually,

And comes again on its circuit.
All the rivers run into the sea,
Yet the sea is not full;
To the place from which the rivers come,
There they return again.
All things are full of labour;
Man cannot express it.
The eye is not satisfied with seeing,
Nor the ear filled with hearing."

and in Ecclesiastes 2:4-11

"I made my works great, I built myself houses, and planted myself vineyards. I made myself gardens and orchards, and I planted all kinds of fruit trees in them. I made myself water pools from which to water the growing trees of the grove. I acquired male and female servants, and had servants born in my house. Yes, I had greater possessions of herds and flocks than all who were in Jerusalem before me. I also gathered for myself silver and gold and the special treasures of kings and of the provinces. I acquired male and female singers, the delights of the sons of men, and musical instruments of all kinds.

So I became great and excelled more than all who were before me in Jerusalem. Also my wisdom remained with me.

Whatever my eyes desired I did not keep from them.
I did not withhold my heart from any pleasure,
For my heart rejoiced in all my labour;
And this was my reward from all my labour.

Then I looked on all the works that my hands had done
And on the labour in which I had toiled;
And indeed all was vanity and grasping for the wind.
There was no profit under the sun."

His attitude towards his life is certainly relatable. There is no point to life if all that you seek is merely physical, and of this natural world that "is passing away" (1 John 2:17). The physical is so temporary, we see this obvious fact in our everyday lives and all around us. Houses require maintenance, food turns rotten if not preserved, electronics malfunction and are continually replaced and upgraded, politicians change regularly, our physical bodies require daily nourishment, buildings can be neglected, and cars require regular maintenance. Nothing that can be seen with the naked eye, lasts. If all you seek in life is to feed your own benefits, desires and needs, comforts and requirements – 'the self' - then you will find that this endeavour ends where its started, with a lie.

LEARNING FROM THE BOOK OF DANIEL

Seduction is the process of deliberately enticing a person, to engage in a relationship, to lead astray, as from duty, rectitude, or the like; to corrupt, to persuade or induce into engaging in sexual behaviour. The world seduces us with too much choice, too much comfort and too much pleasure, making it easy for us to be corrupted by it motives.

The prophet Daniel (620BC – 538BC), from the Old Testament book of Daniel, was also seduced to engage in a relationship or lifestyle that would have distanced him from God had he given into its wiles. He was offered similar things to what king Solomon experienced but knew that cutting these carnal pleasures out, he would be able to remain "sober & vigilant" against its appeal. Daniel was able to withstand what the world put on display and triumph over the same elements that king Solomon eventually suffered emptiness as a result of.

What did Daniel do that allowed him to remain focussed on what God wanted for his life? Do you think that God was pleased with what Daniel did? Do you think that Daniel sought to live within the will of God? What can we learn from Daniel's actions and behaviour about seeking a life after God's heart?

Daniel 1: 3-20

"Then the king instructed Ashpenaz, the master of his eunuchs, to bring some of the children of Israel and some of the king's descendants and some of the nobles, young men in whom there was no blemish, but good-looking, gifted in all wisdom, possessing knowledge and quick to understand, who had ability to serve in the king's palace, and whom they might teach the language and literature of the Chaldeans. And the king appointed for them a daily provision of the king's delicacies and of the wine which he drank, and three years of training for them, so that at the end of that time they might serve before the king. Now from among those of the sons of Judah were Daniel, Hananiah, Mishael, and Azariah. To them the chief of the eunuchs gave names: he gave Daniel the name Belteshazzar; to Hananiah, Shadrach; to Mishael, Meshach; and to Azariah, Abed-Nego.

But Daniel purposed in his heart that he would not defile himself with the portion of the king's delicacies, nor with the wine which he drank; therefore he requested of the chief of the eunuchs that he might not defile himself. Now God had brought Daniel into the favor and goodwill of the chief of the eunuchs. And the chief of the eunuchs said to Daniel, "I fear my lord the king, who has appointed your food and drink. For why should he see your faces looking worse than the young men who are your age? Then you would endanger my head before the king."

So Daniel said to the steward whom the chief of the eunuchs had set over Daniel, Hananiah, Mishael, and Azariah, "Please test your servants for ten days, and let them give us vegetables to eat and water to drink. Then let our appearance be examined before you, and the appearance of the young men who eat the portion of the king's delicacies; and as you see fit, so deal with your servants." So he consented with them in this matter, and tested them ten days.

And at the end of ten days their features appeared better and fatter in flesh than all the young men who ate the portion of the king's delicacies. Thus the steward took away their portion of delicacies and the wine that they were to drink, and gave them vegetables.

As for these four young men, God gave them knowledge and skill in all literature and wisdom; and Daniel had understanding in all visions and dreams.

Now at the end of the days, when the king had said that they should be brought in, the chief of the eunuchs brought them in before Nebuchadnezzar. Then the king interviewed them, and among them all none was found like Daniel, Hananiah, Mishael, and Azariah; therefore they served before the king. And in all matters of wisdom and understanding about which the king examined them, he found them ten times better than all the magicians and astrologers who were in all his realm."

We can apply today what Daniel did in order to remain focussed on the will of God for our lives - they put God before 'self'. The 'self' is prone to temptation and seduction with its main goal to feed its temporary impulses. The men were therefore wise to deny the attractiveness of the palace's pleasures because they understood the weakness of flesh. By rejecting the physical delights that were on offer, they were really rejecting the wiles of the world and so were able to remain "sober and vigilant" (1 Peter 5:8) in the face of distraction. Keeping our minds and bodies clear of what can cause us to let down our guard and be caught unawares, is wisdom. By denying 'the self' (Galatians 5:24), through prayer, modesty, chastening, discipline, fasting and abstinence, Daniel, Hananiah, Mishael, and Azariah were then able to properly carry out what God had purposed for them.

And those *who are* Christ's have crucified the flesh with its passions and desires. – Galatians 5:24

In a modern-day scenario, cutting out the continual onslaught of media, reliance on media, reliance on technology, consumerism, pleasure seeking, indulgent eating and drinking, indulgent living, and convenience are all ways we can diminish the effects of the world's grasp on our hearts and minds. The world's charm can so easily stroke the flesh of 'the self', and seduce it. So just as Daniel, Hananiah,

Mishael, and Azariah, set themselves boundaries and limits in order to flourish, we must do this too.

REVEALING OF ASPECT 2

The second portion of what God revealed to me:

2. Who Jesus truly is

As I wrote previously, words from God come in several dimensions but this particular message was very different because its effect was by far the greatest and most transformational, I have ever experienced. The words "JESUS IS TRUTH" began filling me and gradually increased in intensity over the course of several weeks. The magnitude and weight of the words then took on multiple dimensions where my eyes began opening and the layers of smoky film began peeling away bit-by-bit allowing me to see beyond the natural world and into a perspective from above.

Once these words enveloped my spirit it was then that I saw my body prostrated on the floor of the same house I had been prayed for. To prostrate is to throw oneself flat on the ground, lying face downwards, especially in submission or reverence - only I didn't throw myself down - *I was knocked over, in spirit.*

The awesome value, the immense weight, and the piercing consequence of the statement above is ineffable. To say that something is ineffable is to say that it is too great or extreme to be expressed or described in human words. Only the Spirit of God can reveal the answer to you. *How then do I convey this indescribable unhuman experience to others? How difficult is this going to be, if I can't even express with words what God has communicated to me?*

CANDACE ANNE

HUMBLY TRYING TO EXPLAIN

*O Lord God, I humble myself before You. With my ability and
opportunity to share this story in writing – please help me do
justice to what you have allowed me to experience. My hope
is that when others read and hear this story, they too may be
opened to the Truth and desire close communion with You.*

In the name of Your Holy Anointed Son Jesus Christ. Amen

In a series of points, I will attempt to elaborate in human words what
God communicated to me in spirit. *How can I possibly give justice to what
God allowed me to see using mere English? How can I possibly relay its full
message?* My eyes tear up as I write this because I am so humbled that
the imperfect and flawed me can be used as an instrument to share
something so remarkable about His Kingdom. *I really do, I really try
to love the* LORD *my God with all my heart, with all my soul, and with all
my mind, and with all my strength, because of this I am deeply and humbly
moved to be able to share this with you. I hope I can do the message justice.*

Here goes.

What I *received*:

- **Truth = completion, fullness, exact, fulfilment, perfection, highest form**

- **The Truth emanates from Good, God the Father**

  Emanates: (of a feeling, quality, or sensation) issue or spread
  out from (a source), originate from; be produced by, give out
  or emit (a feeling, quality, or sensation)).

- **Jesus and Truth cannot be separated – they are inextricably linked**

Inextricable: in a way that is impossible to disentangle or separate.

- **Jesus is the perfect expression of God's image. He is God's ultimate expression of fullness. He is fully Divine and fully human – He is full and whole.**

- **Jesus is the reason for and behind creation – He is the reason for everything**

- **There is no lie in Truth, no darkness at all**

- **The Truth opposes the world and its constructs**

- **Jesus is the perfect unity of flesh and Spirit**

- **Jesus is the perfect unity of Law and Grace – He is perfect Law – He is perfect Grace = He is perfect Love = He is perfect**

God has spoken to humanity through Scripture, which is His eternal and living past revelation to us, as well as through His Holy Spirit who guides and helps us today. So, when Scripture and Spirit coincide, the message being given is accurate because there has been one mindedness.

For example: weeks before I was set to fly out to South Africa alone with my five-year-old daughter in 2019 for a short trip, there was a period of four days where I was continuously pressed with the following words: "Lord go before me", "Lord go before me", "Lord go before me", "Lord go before me". Eventually I couldn't leave it any longer and had to find out what they meant because I'd never heard this phrase before and didn't know where this unusual continuous urge to say these words was coming from. Eventually, on the fourth day of receiving and then praying these words before any situation I would encounter, I sat down at my computer and did some research.

Immediately up popped the answer, **"And the LORD, He *is* the One who goes before you. He will be with you, He will not leave you nor forsake you; do not fear nor be dismayed"** (Deuteronomy 31:8). Well, I couldn't believe it! Right then and there I realised what had been happening and started crying. *What an incredible moment!*

God had actually breathed words from Scripture into my spirit. I couldn't believe it! Words that Moses used when speaking to Joshua, who was soon to become the new leader of Israel and lead the Israelites across the Jordan, roughly around the years 1300 BC were given to insignificant little ol' me in 2019 AD. That is roughly 3320 years apart. I was speechless! *Why had He done that?* How great is our God! The God of the universe yet at the same time, the God of our heart. So immense, yet so intimate.

How transcendent (existing apart from and not subject to the limitations of the material universe) **are His Words.** They reach from the beginning of time until the end, wow! "Likewise the Spirit also helps in our weaknesses. For we do not know what we should pray for as we ought, but the Spirit Himself makes intercession for us with groanings which cannot be uttered. Now He who searches the hearts knows what the mind of the Spirit *is,* because He makes intercession for the saints according to *the will of* God" (Romans 8:26-27).

How living and active is His Word. "For the word of God *is* living and powerful, and sharper than any two-edged sword, piercing even to the division of soul and spirit, and of joints and marrow, and is a discerner of the thoughts and intents of the heart" (Hebrews 4:12).

This experience has definitely become one of my most memorable moments in my journey of faith. Firstly, because it *was* the Holy Spirit and not my own thoughts continuously pressing me with the words, and secondly because they aligned perfectly with Scripture and thirdly, God was giving me assurance and peace that everything would be okay while on my trip, and even beyond that. The message I received over the course of those four days was therefore completely true.

Therefore, because Jesus says of Himself: "I am the truth" (John 14:6), I know that the message I received, "JESUS IS TRUTH", is accurate because that message was given to me by the Holy Spirit and is also found already in Scripture.

- **The Truth is the beginning and the end**

  The Hebrew word for *truth* is *Emmet*, spelled Alpeh/Mem/Tav (אמת). We find that **truth** was, is, and is to come. The three letters that make up the **word** Emmet are the beginning (א), middle (מ), and the end (ת) letters of the **Hebrew** alphabet (words in Hebrew are read from right to left). The morphology (how a word is formed) of the word *truth* itself, therefore holds within it the beginning, the middle and the end of what makes up the entire verbal communicative portion of our being: language, in this case the Hebrew language. Because language is an inborn and inherited characteristic in human beings bestowed on as image bearers when we were first created in God's Image (Genesis 1:26-27), how words themselves are formed is not chance but absolutely intentional and subject to the designer's design.

  Emmet means the whole truth: beginning, middle and end, and this meaning is based on the word itself and its relation to the Hebrew Alphabet. Truth is not just one piece of the truth, but the whole thing, beginning, middle and end. If some part of the truth is left out, then it is not really the truth.

  Jesus says: "I am the Alpha and the Omega, *the* Beginning and *the* End, the First and the Last" (Revelations 22:13), "I am the Root and the Offspring of David, the Bright and Morning Star" (Revelations 22:16), "the author and finisher of *our* faith" (Hebrews 12:2) and "I am the truth" (John 14:16). How can someone possibly be the beginning of something and the end of something, or both the predecessor and descendant at the same time? Jesus must then be both the foundation and the peak.

"He is the image of the invisible God, the firstborn over all creation. For by Him all things were created that are in heaven and that are on earth, visible and invisible, whether thrones or dominions or principalities or powers. All things were created through Him and for Him. And He is before all things, and in Him all things consist. And He is the head of the body, the church, who is the beginning, the firstborn from the dead, that in all things He may have the pre-eminence" (Colossians 1:15-17). Again, how can He be the firstborn over all creation and firstborn from the dead? The answer - only if He is the *blueprint* for life itself. In simple: He is the truth.

- **Old version obliterated**

The understanding I had about who Jesus Christ was *before* I experienced the revelation I did has been blown out of the water and obliterated into smithereens when compared to the knowledge I have about Him now. The revelation I received expressed to me who He *actually* is. It was like an answer as large as our planet – not only an *outer body* experience, like when I saw my own body prostrated on the floor of a house, but an *outer planetary* one, if I could describe it like that. My perspective about all life on earth was dramatically impacted. I saw the world from another *realm* of understanding, from a non-human perspective I'd say. I saw the pride of the world, the pride of life, and that Jesus is in none of that. No detailed sentences were provided with lists of explanations on what I needed to know but rather I experienced a full body outer world sensory awakening that completely transformed my viewpoint about how the world was created, what my purpose is and what the purpose of life is.

The best Biblical reference that explains what I experienced are the passages in the book of Acts where Saul of Tarsus was confronted with who Jesus *really is*. The belief He had previously of who Jesus was, was flattened after hearing directly from Him.

During the time when Saul encountered the resurrected Christ, Saul was working his way up the ranks in the Jewish synagogue, being very zealous in trying to maintain strict Jewish law and persecute those who disobeyed the Old Testament laws and Jewish customs. Many Jews at the time didn't understand that Jesus was the Messiah, and anybody who claimed to be the Son of God was considered to be blaspheming and could be put to death under the Jewish law that Saul was trying to defend. But one day while on his way to Damascus (capital of Syria today) to actually search for and persecute more followers of "the Way" (men and women who followed Jesus), he met with Jesus Christ Himself.

Acts 9: 1-9

"Then Saul, still breathing threats and murder against the disciples of the Lord, went to the high priest and asked letters from him to the synagogues of Damascus, so that if he found any who were of the Way, whether men or women, he might bring them bound to Jerusalem.

As he journeyed he came near Damascus, and suddenly a light shone around him from heaven. Then he fell to the ground, and heard a voice saying to him, "Saul, Saul, why are you persecuting Me?" And he said, "Who are You, Lord? Then the Lord said, "I am Jesus, whom you are persecuting. It is hard for you to kick against the goads."

So he, trembling and astonished, said, "Lord, what do You want me to do?"

Then the Lord said to him, "Arise and go into the city, and you will be told what you must do."

And the men who journeyed with him stood speechless, hearing a voice but seeing no one. Then Saul arose from the ground, and when his eyes were opened he saw no one. But they led him by the hand and brought him into Damascus. And he was three days without sight, and neither ate nor drank."

After Saul encountered the truth about Jesus, who He *actually* is, he was transformed. Transformed into a new person with a new heart and new mind. Later he became known as the Apostle Paul and in turn wrote most of the New Testament epistles. He also founded several churches in Asia Minor and Europe and taught the gospel of Christ to the first century Christians. From a murderer to a disciple – only God can transform like this. Being directly spoken to by Jesus, who wasn't even physically present in that moment, and having the truth revealed to like that with the truth of who He is, transformed Paul's understanding that no other means could have done. Paul must have thought Jesus was dead, and then he heard from Him from Heaven, no learning or studying would have achieved this is as effectively as a direct encounter with Christ Himself. Jesus didn't even say much in the above passage, but in *spirit*, Paul was ministered to in such a powerful way, a way mysteriously hidden in God, he could do nothing else but surrender and convert. Paul was going one way and then encountered *the Truth* and with the already acquired knowledge and teaching of Scripture, together it came alive and Paul's purpose shifted, causing him to be "born again".

I would never want to equate or presume to liken my experience to the Apostle Paul's because his conversion helped shaped the entire Christian faith but I can definitely relate in part to his spiritual awakening. I can relate to how it completely transformed his purpose, viewpoint of life, his understanding of who Jesus *actually is*, and his understanding of good and evil. My entire being was shifted into another dimension of awareness of these aspects causing me to realise things I had never before.

Firstly, was the realisation of who Jesus *actually* is, Him being the reason for everything. Even though I had always believed that Jesus was the Son of God, and that what He said and did in the New Testament was true, I still only knew these truths in my head and on paper. But after my spiritual awakening all this information turned into a clear black-and-white unveiled reality which transformed all of me, and my heart. Before, I had the Sunday school picture book version, the baby in the manger during Christmas version, the crucified on the cross version, and the version in whose name we pray, but now, I have the unwavering knowledge of the heart and mind – something no one else can shake.

Another aspect of Paul's conversion that is poignantly meaningful to me is that after his encounter with Christ, he was blinded for three days. I have no doubt that after being spoken to in the midst of heavenly light streaming from heaven, one would be awestruck and completely humbled, but to go completely blind for three days and then released of that blindness is also astounding. Paul's blindness is significant for all of us because in his blindness he was veiled, but when *the Truth* overcame Him, the truth about who Jesus really is, he experienced the unveiling. "But their minds were blinded. For until this day the same veil remains unlifted in the reading of the Old Testament, because the veil is taken away in Christ. But even to this day, when Moses is read, a veil lies on their heart. Nevertheless when one turns to the Lord, the veil is taken away. Now the Lord is the Spirit; and where the Spirit of the Lord is, there is liberty" (2 Corinthians 3: 14-17). Paul's mind was blinded in the law, but *Jesus as Truth* removed his blindness and opened his eyes.

I TOO WAS BLIND

John Newton's (1725–1807) timeless lyrics to the famous hymn *Amazing Grace,* attest to what happened to Paul on the road to Damascus in 1st century AD. In his own conversion in 1748 during a violent sea storm, he cried out to God for mercy and his cry was heard. John was involved in the Atlantic Slave Trade and after *the Truth* opened his eyes, he later became an abolitionist. The words, "Was blind, but now I see" ring true for both these men, Paul and John, in that they were heading in one direction, but when they encountered *the Truth*, they turned around and away from under the veil. *The Truth* set both these men free.

Amazing Grace by John Newton (1779)

1. Amazing grace! How sweet the sound
    That saved a wretch like me!
    I once was lost, but now am found;
    Was blind, but now I see.

2. 'Twas grace that taught my heart to fear,
    And grace my fears relieved;
    How precious did that grace appear
    The hour I first believed.

3. Through many dangers, toils, and snares,
    I have already come;
    'Tis grace hath brought me safe thus far,
    And grace will lead me home.

4. The Lord has promised good to me,
    His Word my hope secures;
    He will my Shield and Portion be,
    As long as life endures.

5.   Yea, when this flesh and heart shall fail,
And mortal life shall cease,
I shall possess, within the veil,
A life of joy and peace.

6.   The earth shall soon dissolve like snow,
The sun forbear to shine;
But God, who called me here below,
Will be forever mine.

7.   When we've been there ten thousand years,
Bright shining as the sun,
We've no less days to sing God's praise
Than when we'd first begun.

•   **The blood of the Lamb**

One of the most superb visual representations of how Christ's sacrificial death affected Satan's plan for humanity [the plan to eternally separate us from God / to split us from God's presence *(diabaline (devil) – to split)],* is depicted in the Mel Gibson directed American Biblical drama, *Passion of the Christ* (2004). Another film that must be watched.

The moment when Christ dies and utters the words, "It is finished" (John 19:30), Christ's purpose for which He was sent to earth was accomplished.

Christ came to destroy the work of Satan, which is to lead and keep men and women away from God, i.e., to sin against / to live separately from God. Satan continues to work at keeping people's eyes covered and ignorant of their sin (through distraction and deception), with his ultimate goal of trying to eternally separate us from God.

He who sins is of the devil, for the devil has sinned from the beginning. For this purpose the Son of God was manifested, that He might destroy the works of the devil. - 1 John 3:8

Cinematically, the film depicts Satan's agony impeccably during the moment where he realises that Jesus is finally dead and that a blood sacrifice has been made. The camera films Satan's screaming face whilst on his knees in a barren dried up piece of earth and then zooms out further with him still writhing in anguish. Because Christ has just died, blood has been shed, which to a righteous God is payment for sins committed. Throughout the Old Testament, sacrificial blood was used to atone for sins. God is so just and righteous that only innocent blood can atone/make amends with Him. *Atonement is the way that humans are reconciled (brought back) to God.* Jesus Christ made atonement (made a way back to God) on our behalf by giving His sacrificial blood, instead of ours, so that we have the means to be reconciled back to God - just as we were before *the fall*. Only what is washed clean and without blemish can be in the presence of a Holy God and sin stains our appearance to God.

And I said to him, "Sir, you know," So he said to me, "These are the ones who come out of the great tribulation, and washed their robes and made them white in the blood of the Lamb. - Revelation 7:14

For what the law could not do in that it was weak through the flesh, God did by sending His own Son in the likeness of sinful flesh, on account of sin: He condemned sin in the flesh, that the righteous requirement of the law might be fulfilled in us who do not walk according to the flesh but according to the Spirit. For those who live according to the flesh set their minds on the things of the flesh, but those who live according to the Spirit, the things of the Spirit. For to be carnally minded is death, but to be spiritually minded is life and peace. Because the carnal mind is enmity against

God; for it is not subject to the law of God, nor indeed can be. So then, those who are in the flesh cannot please God. - Romans 8:3-8

PASSOVER » THE BLOOD OF THE LAMB

As the Bible is both a work of literary genius and prophecy, the Bible is full of foreshadowing. *Foreshadowing is a literary device in which a writer hints in advance of what is to come later in the story. Foreshadowing mostly appears at the beginning of a story, or chapter, and helps the reader build expectations of what might transpire.* Mirroring the Old Testament book of Exodus when God executed judgment against Egypt (Exodus 12:12) is the death of Jesus in the New Testament. After the ninth plague and just before the worst one of all, the Jewish people were instructed to use the blood of a lamb and wipe it onto the two doorposts and on the lintel of the houses (Exodus 12:7). This was instructed to be done so that the plague of death would not strike their families, by passing over them – hence the name 'Passover'. The Lord said, "… the blood shall be a sign for you on the houses where you are. And when I see the blood, I will pass over you; and the plague shall not be on you to destroy you when I strike the land of Egypt" (Exodus 12:13).

JUDGMENT OF DEATH

The tenth plague was death. "The Lord said: 'About midnight I will go out into the midst of Egypt; all the firstborn in the land of Egypt shall die, from the firstborn of Pharaoh who sits on his throne, even to the firstborn of the female servant who is behind the hand mill, and all the firstborn of the animals. Then there shall be a great cry throughout all the land of Egypt, such as was not like it before, nor shall be like it again. But against none of the children of Israel shall a dog move its tongue, against man or beast, that you may know that the LORD does make a difference between the *Egyptians and *Israel"

(Exodus 11:4-7). This act of the Lord became known as the Passover where only with the blood of the lamb, did death pass over the house and not strike the household. In the same way that the blood of the lamb saved the people of Israel against death, the blood of *the Lamb* will save us from eternal death. *Thank you, Jesus.*

OLD AND NEW LINKED

The masterfully woven tapestry of the Old and New Testament that is the Bible, is so skilfully written and composed that it is by far the most superb piece of written work on earth because it was written through the power of the Holy Spirit. Words spoken thousands of years apart are connected and mirrored so awesomely, with the pages bursting with symbolism and relevance, connectivity and meaning.

When Abraham (Genesis 22:1-19), who was alive on earth thousands of years before the blood of Jesus was given as a sacrifice, was confronted with sacrificing his only beloved son and when asked by Isaac, his son, before the moment of sacrifice, "Where is the lamb for the burnt offering?" Abraham replied and said, "My son, God will provide himself a lamb for the burnt offering." Centuries later God did provide the lamb, in the way of His only beloved begotten Son (John 3:16), as Abraham's words foreshadowing what would transpire one day. Isaac also didn't challenge his father because he himself surrendered to God's will, just as Jesus willingly understood the work He had to do and what He came to complete. "For God so loved the world that He gave His only begotten Son, that whoever believes in Him should not perish but have everlasting life" (John 3:16).

Therefore, the Old is essential for grasping the New. Both testimonies, equally valuable and equally applicable, are vital in realising and seeing the whole truth.

BACK TO THE FILM

In the Garden of Gethsemane scene in the *Passion of the Christ* (2004), before the character of Jesus (played by Jim Caviezel) is apprehended by the Roman soldiers, the character who plays Satan, scornfully questions the character of Jesus whether He really believes that one man can bear the full burden of sin? Jesus responds in the film by praying to His Father for strength to endure what He knows awaits Him. Satan then temptingly challenges the character of Jesus by saying that no one can carry this burden. It is far too heavy and costly to save their souls. No one could ever do it.

Just this conversation between Jesus (played by Jim Caviezel) and Satan (played by Rosalinda Celentano) illustrates the worth and weight of the sacrifice that Jesus is about to submit to. In the film, Jesus is about to make a way for any man or woman to reach God, with the payment of His innocent blood for the wages of sin that Satan caused *us* (Garden of Eden) to commit in the first place. Jesus allowed us to become clean before God, "… and washed their robes and made them white in the blood of the Lamb" (Revelations 7:14). *What love!*

Obviously, Satan doesn't want this to happen which is why Satan makes one final attempt in the film at tempting Jesus with doubt. Satan hates Jesus because of who He is. Jesus is *the Truth* to eternal life and Satan is the complete opposite, a lie.

Jesus is the way to eternal life; Satan is the way to eternal death.

When viewing this film after my eyes had been *opened*, Christ's sacrifice and the severity of it started making perfect and mesmerizing sense.

CHOICE BETWEEN LIFE AND DEATH

However, just like the angels, humans have been given free will. Free will (because none of us are robots) to choose between *a life of life* and *a life of death* because "death and life *are* in the power of the tongue" (Proverbs 18:21). Even though God ultimately decides in the end, one must confess with one's tongue that you accept the sacrifice that Jesus made for your sin as payment to a righteous God.

Because we're sinners, and since sin separates us from God, without Christ's atonement one cannot see Heaven. Christ's blood was shed for us to be able to stand in the presence of God, just like we first did before *the fall* in Eden. If not, you will face the *same* judgment as the angels who were cast from Heaven for sinning against God. "Depart from Me, you cursed, into the everlasting fire prepared for the devil and his angels" (Matthew 25:41), and "... go away into everlasting punishment, but the righteous into eternal life" (Matthew 25:46).

Unfortunately, yet seriously, there will be those who will not accept but deny what Christ has done for them and when He returns to earth "in His glory, and all the holy angels with Him" (Matthew 25:31), to judge the nations, He will separate His true followers from those who have denied Him. "All the nations will be gathered before Him, and He will separate them one from another, as a shepherd divides *his* sheep from the goats" (Matthew 25:32).

The New Testament book of Ephesians reminds us that there was a time when only the people of Israel (the Jewish nation) could be accepted by God and all the other nations were "aliens from the commonwealth of Israel and strangers from the covenants of promise, having no hope and without God in the world. But now in Christ Jesus you who once were far off have been brought near by the blood of Christ" (Ephesians 2:11-13). The blood of Jesus has made it possible for every human being, not only the Jewish people, to have eternal life. What glorious news this is, that Christ's love surpasses all race, boundary, ethnicity, and physical element. To this I say, *HALLELUJAH! THANK YOU, JESUS!*

IN WHOSE NAME

Surely I will pour out my spirit on you; I will make my words known to you. – Proverbs 1:23

I remember a particular moment when the statement, "Only what is done for Christ will last" resonated with me. I had been grappling with my future plans for the year ahead and like many of my conversations with God, this one also took place in a vehicle. As I pulled into the driveway at home in South Africa, opened the car door and stepped out, a string of *words flowed* over me once again, and it was an answer to the unspoken prayer I'd been having. They were, "Only what is done for Christ will last". That was it, just those words, "Only what is done for Christ will last". *Wow!*

Only what is done in the name of Jesus has any effect on your everlasting future. All the charities you donate to, all the club memberships you are a part of, all the offices you hold and committees you serve on, none of the labour makes any difference if it's not done to advance the Kingdom of God on earth. If it is not done to uplift, honour and glorify the person and work of Jesus Christ and *His Truth*, then it does not last past this life on earth. Yes, it's decent and rewarding to give, donate and volunteer, but once I discovered that Jesus is the Truth of life, the direction of my life's purpose and motives for my actions changed. My mission is for Him now.

"Not everyone who says to Me, 'Lord, Lord,' shall enter the kingdom of heaven, but he who does the will of My Father in heaven. Many will say to Me in that day, 'Lord, Lord, have we not

prophesied in Your name, cast out demons in Your name, and done many wonders in Your name?' And then I will declare to them, 'I never knew you; depart from Me, you who practice lawlessness!'

CONFIRMED BY SCRIPTURE

I broke down and cried one night when reading aloud to someone else from the book of Colossians because the message I had received during those three months of awakening was already right there in the book I was holding. Everything I now understood about Jesus, had already been written down two thousand ago in the book of Colossians 1:15-20, only now it had become real and personal for me. The words on paper had come alive and were breathing life into me.

Colossians 1:15-20

"He is the image of the invisible God, the firstborn over all creation. For by Him all things were created that are in heaven and that are on earth, visible and invisible, whether thrones or dominions or principalities or powers. All things were created through Him and for Him. And He is before all things, and in Him all things consist. And He is the head of the body, the church, who is the beginning, the firstborn from the dead, that in all things He may have the pre-eminence.

For it pleased the Father that in Him all the fullness should dwell, and by Him to reconcile all things to Himself, by Him, whether things on earth or things in heaven, having made peace through the blood of His cross."

WHAT IS TRUTH?

"Jesus is Truth" were the audible words I heard and experienced deeply, as well as a deep unfolding realisation of what this actually means.

"What is truth?" I have been asked, "How can Jesus be Truth?", "What does that even mean?", "What does truth mean?" I have been asked again and again. With the knowledge I had received combined with what is already written in Colossians, I'll explain what I realised, as well as with an illustration that I drew.

"... image of the invisible God, the firstborn over all creation." – begotten of the Father. "No one has seen God at any time. The only begotten Son, who is in the bosom of the Father, He has declared Him" (John 1:18). The *Truth* emanates / springs from / proceeds forth / originates from God the Father, who is Good. The *Truth* emanates from Good.

"For by Him all things were created that are in heaven and that are on earth, visible and invisible, ..." – through *Truth*, God created the world. Through Jesus, all things were created. "All things were made through Him, and without Him nothing was made that was made" (John 1:3). "For since the creation of the world His invisible *attributes* are clearly seen, being understood by the things that are made, even His eternal power and Godhead, so that they are without excuse" (Romans 1:20).

"All things were created through Him and for Him." Jesus is the reason for it all. He is reason for creation itself. Everything was created for Him, as His dominion and inheritance as the heir. "God, who at various times and in various ways spoke in time past to the fathers by the prophets, has in these last days spoken to us by *His* Son, whom He has appointed heir of all things, through whom also He made the worlds ..." (Hebrews 1:1-2).

"He is before all things, and in Him all things consist". Jesus *was* before the world began. "And now, O Father, glorify Me together with Yourself, with the glory which I had with You before the world was" (John 17:5). Consist *means to be composed or made up of,* which means that the world itself and everything in it, is the Lord's (Psalm 24:1). *Truth* is the very make-up of all things, it is the framework, the foundation, the mechanism, the founding principle, how it works, how it functions perfectly, how it was meant to function, its ultimate purpose for good, the very blueprint. For example: a simple rose was created through *Truth*. This *Truth* is perfect knowledge: it is the intricate perfect biology of it, the perfect design of it, the perfect science of it, the perfect aesthetic of it, the perfect purpose of it – it is perfect because the *Truth* is perfect.

"And He is the head of the body, the church, who is the beginning," Jesus is the head of the body of believers, all who believe and give witness to His testimony. We the believers are the hands and feet on earth of the supernatural body of Christ. When Christ was resurrected, the church of Christ was born.

"the firstborn from the dead, that in all things He may have the pre-eminence". Jesus is the firstborn of the dead, the resurrection and the life (John 11:25). He is perfected resurrection and perfected life. He is the perfect example of life. "Because I live, you will live also" (John 14:19). Jesus is the truth to life.

In all things, since Jesus is the *Truth*, He has the supremacy and excellence. For example: the beautiful song of a bird chirping in the trees demonstrates the simplicity of *Truth*. The perfect bio'logy' (structure, function, growth, origin, adaptation and distribution of living organisms) of the bird fulfilling its exact purpose for which it was created, demonstrates *Truth*. Truth is how it is. Truth is perfect biology, perfect aesthetic, perfect form. We see Christ's Truth in all the created world because the Truth created the world. *Truth* shows us what's *Good*.

"that in Him all the fullness should dwell" *Truth* is the absolute highest form of life. Truth is absolute. Truth is Christ, and everything is complete in Him.

"and by Him to reconcile all things to Himself, by Him, whether things on earth or things in heaven, having made peace through the blood of His cross." Through *Truth* we reach Good, through Jesus we reach God the Father. "For this *is* good and acceptable in the sight of God our Saviour, who desires all men to be saved and to come to the knowledge of the truth. For *there is* one God and one Mediator between God and men, *the* Man Christ Jesus, who gave Himself a ransom for all, to be testified in due time, for which I was appointed a preacher and an apostle—I am speaking the truth in Christ *and* not lying—a teacher of the Gentiles in faith and truth" (1 Timothy 2:3-7).

EXPLAINING THE ILLUSTRATION

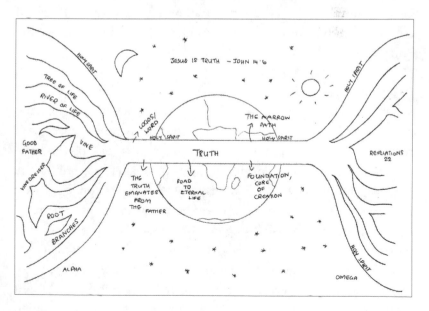

When asked to illustrate *What is Truth*, the above drawing emerged with a particular focus on how "All things were created through Him and for Him".

In the illustration, the Truth / Jesus / Son bares the "image of the invisible God" and like the "streams of living water" (John 7:38) and the "river of the water of life, clear as crystal, coming from the throne of God and of the Lamb" (Revelations 22:1), the *Truth* and the Life flows from Good and through this *Truth*, "all things were created", and only through this *Truth* is eternal life and only through this Truth can one be reconciled to God the Father.

The semi-circle on the left represents the God-head (Father, Son & Holy Spirit), the Good in the centre with *Truth* flowing out from the Good like the branches of a tree and streams of life across the page to the right. Interestingly, because of the A4 page I drew the image on, the God-head is not closed because God has no limits. We also don't understand or know the fullness of God so the unintentional open ended semi-circle illustrates this quite well.

In the background of the illustration (between the semi-circles) we see the "heavens and the earth" (Genesis 1:1), behind the "narrow path" of *Truth* (Matthew 7:13-14) demonstrating that the *Truth* created the world and everything in it. This narrow path or ribbon in the illustration somehow beautifully and appropriately resembles the narrow path written about in Matthew 7:13-14 where Jesus says that the way to life is narrow. This narrowness was unintentional but is what emerged when visualising how to explain *What is Truth?* to a persistent questioning friend, of which I am very thankful for because their wrestling is what pushed me to communicate the message more plainly and visually. When explaining verbally, sometimes in heated discussion with my persistent friend, I would see a glowing orange ribbon moving away from me as the viewer in a forward motion across a pitch-black expanse of nothingness. It was almost like a flat ribbon of fiery orange glowing light projecting through an empty black (no stars and no planets) universe. This particular drawing is what the *vision* looks like from a side view. *Truth* running through from the beginning right to the end.

Wonderfully, the drawing also displays how *Jesus as the Truth* is "the Alpha and the Omega, *the* Beginning and *the* End, the First and the Last" (Revelations 22:13), with the *Truth* proceeding from the beginning and "before the world was" all the way to the end of the age, and beyond into eternity. The creation of the heavens and the earth is also depicted as mentioned in Genesis 1:1, as well as the end which will be the end of the age when the Lord returns as mentioned in Matthew 24. At the third quarter of the page though is where my *vision or understanding or revelation* stopped, so I can't explain anything about 'the end'. All I know is that we eagerly await in expectant hope for the return of our Lord Jesus Christ, "For our citizenship is in heaven, from which we also eagerly wait for the Saviour, the Lord Jesus Christ" (Phillipians 3:20).

The narrow strip running across the heavens and the earth also references John 14:6 where Jesus says, "I am the way, the truth, and the life. No one comes to the Father except through Me." Only through this way of *Truth*, walking *in Truth* on earth, can one be reconciled to God. "I have no greater joy than to hear that my children walk in truth" (3 John 1:4). To walk the narrow path on earth is to walk in the way of *Truth*, this means knowing and keeping the gospel and testimony of Christ as your basis for defining your beliefs. As your identity lies in Him, your definitions lie in Him, how you define things are determined by who Christ is and what Christ taught.

One of the ways to walk in the *Truth* is to reject the lie that the world throws at you, "... wide is the gate and broad is the road that leads to destruction, and many enter through it" (Matthew 7:13). This denial of the world's seduction is done with the help of the Holy Spirit who is the Spirit of Truth, as He convicts us of what is good and what is evil. "The Spirit of truth, whom the world cannot receive, because it neither sees Him nor knows Him; but you know Him, for He dwells with you and will be in you" (John 14:17).

One example of what is inside this narrow strip of *Truth* is God's definition of marriage. This being the union between one man and one woman. Anything outside these defined parameters that God has created, is outside *Truth* and a lie. Lies are from Satan and lead to destruction, and will leave you outside the "belt of truth" (Ephesians 6:14)).

Interestingly, the narrow strip also resembles a bridge, with Jesus being the bridge between God and us. "For *there is* one God and one Mediator between God and men, *the* Man Christ Jesus" (1 Timothy 2:5), "And for this reason He is the Mediator of the new covenant, by means of death, for the redemption of the transgressions under the first covenant, that those who are called may receive the promise of the eternal inheritance" (Hebrews 9:15).

Jesus is the *Truth* and through Him as *Truth* the world was created, but also for Him the world was created. After my *revelation*, I understood that everything is for Jesus and only what is done for Him will last. "God, who at various times and in various ways spoke in time past to the fathers by the prophets, has in these last days spoken to us by *His* Son, whom He has appointed heir of all things, through whom also He made the worlds; who being the brightness of *His* glory and the express image of His person, and upholding all things by the word of His power, when He had by Himself purged our sins, sat down at the right hand of the Majesty on high, having become so much better than the angels, as He has by inheritance obtained a more excellent name than they" (Hebrews 1: 1-4).

God *is* Spirit, and those who worship Him must worship in spirit and truth. – John 4:24.

See also: John 14:6, John 4:24, John 7:38, Jeremiah 17:13, John 4:10, Revelation 7:17, Proverbs 11:30, Proverbs 15:4, Revelation 2:7, Revelation 22:14, Isaiah 11:10, Genesis 1:2, John 15:26.

- My favourite Bible teachers so far are David Pawson and Derek Prince, even just listening to their voices on audio is calming. David Pawson brought up an interesting concept in one of his many online sermons I've had the privilege of listening to. He introduced to my ears the word "logos", and when he began his explanation, I surprisingly understood exactly what he meant even though I had never heard the word before. The Greek word "logos" has been translated into the English word as "Word", however the Greek definition of the word is much more extensive than its diluted English version.

Just as the full impact of the Greek word *agape* - the *highest form* of love and *the love of God* - is lost when you translate it into the English as 'love', so is the full meaning of "logos" lost and diluted when translated into the younger English language. The richness and fullness of both these Greek words are weakened, sadly giving us a watered-down version of their far-reaching expanse and what they truly mean. When one skips over the original cause of a word, one loses understanding of it. By missing out on the cause of it, you are essentially not being communicated to properly. For this reason, it is imperative to study the older translations of the Bible, especially the Hebrew and Greek form because the original intention of the message is much clearer.

When we look at what "logos" means in the original Greek, we start understanding more of why Jesus was referred to as "logos". During those three months of my *spiritual awakening* in 2016, this concept of "logos" is exactly what I grasped. The miraculous part of it though is that I had never acquired any theoretical knowledge on this subject prior, but was shown and transported *in spirit* into a deep understanding of this concept.

Logos therefore can be explained as: *"the incarnate utterance of God", "God's very breath of life", "emanating from the core of God", "representing the fullness of God's glory", "God's transcendent power", "a manifestation of thinking and doing", "communicating the way and will of God to the world", "perfect in knowledge, insight and judgment", "foundation of all knowledge: -'logy'", "foundation of all what is seen and unseen", "the core values of creation", and "the bridge between man and God".*

Take for example the branch of knowledge known as biology. Biology is the science of life. Its name is derived from the Greek words "bios" (life) and "logos" (study). Biology *is* the structure, function, growth, origin, adaptation and distribution of living organisms, and the *Truth* formed every aspect of it. How an animal breathes and functions and grows and reproduces and lives and adapts is all designed in *Truth*. When one studies an area such as biology, one is actually studying how 'life' was designed and pieced together, i.e., the core foundation, framework, cornerstone, pinnacle of creation – the actual formula.

People quickly forget that when they are studying an area of creation, they are actually uncovering the *Truth*: uncovering Jesus.

The book of John opens with, "In the beginning was the Word, and the Word was with God, and the Word was God" (John 1:1). When you replace the word "Word" with "Logos" you get an entirely renewed understanding of who John understood Jesus to be. Logos = Truth = Jesus.

New identity: after & going forward

"The purpose of your life is far greater than your own personal fulfilment, your peace of mind, or even your happiness. It's far greater than your family, your career, or even your wildest dreams and ambitions. If you want to know why you were placed on this planet, you must begin with God. You were born by his purpose and for his purpose." – Rick Warren, *The Purpose Driven Life*

Ever meet a complete stranger at the park or on the bus, strike up a conversation, chat for ages and when your conversation's over, go your separate ways feeling entirely refreshed and inspired yet not even exchanging numbers in order to meet up again? Not because you didn't want to, but because you both just knew that your meet-up was a once-off lovely chance encounter you shared - and that was it. This has happened to me several times but there is one conversation in particular that stands out above the rest.

The day was warm and the skies were clear, so as a family we headed out to South Bank parklands in Brisbane to spend the day at the pools and beach. Soon after arriving I found a comfortable spot on the rocks from where to watch my husband and daughter enjoy their swim, while my son slept in the pram next to me. Soon another family began swimming close by with the mom also watching from the side-lines, just as I was. It wasn't long before I detected a familiar accent which made for an instant ice-breaker.

At first, we chatted about the usual surface-level topics like immigration, schools, families and jobs until eventually we got onto the subject matter for which we were both actually there and the real reason behind our serendipitous encounter - identity.

Once we discovered that we were both Christians, our guards dropped and the friendly chat we were having turned into a heart-to-heart one. Because we had both left our countries of origin and had now embarked on the journey of settling into a new one, we started discussing our identities with respects to our culture, heritage and language, and how these aspects figure into our new lives in a completely different region of the world. *As it's easier to identify with people of the same culture and language, how do we now identify with people who don't share the same culture or heritage?* It was then that she confirmed what I had also been feeling: "My culture, heritage and language now come second to my identity as a disciple of the Lord. I am a Christian first before anything else," she said. I looked at her with approving eyes and absorbed every word of our discussion.

Not too long afterwards, her kids exited the pool and so we said our good-byes, but it was entirely okay because we had received what we needed to receive from each other. That unplanned encounter was not so unplanned I believe, because those words still impress on me today and I truly believe there was a greater purpose for us meeting.

How wonderful that a random chance encounter could make such an impact. This conversation was exactly what I needed to hear at that time. *Only God knew that.*

IDENTITY IN CHRIST

What does it mean to have your identity in Christ?

What does it mean when you say I identify with Christ or that my identity is in Jesus?

What does it mean when you say my identity lies in *Truth?*

BEFORE V NOW

If I compare *my identity* or *who and what I identified with* before my realisation of who Jesus is, to now, I clearly see how contrasting they are. I was trying to identify with Hollywood, what I saw on TV and what I saw in magazines. From relationships to career decisions, from who I admired to who I desired to become like. All of these ambitions were mostly centred on media portrayals of characters written by another person who most likely had their definitions written by a worldly standard.

There is *absolute Truth* in who and what I identify with now, compared to the *lie* I identified with back then. I thought I could find peace and answers to life but still have my motives, ambitions, values, and purpose driven by what the world valued and deemed acceptable. I spent years and years tearing between these two-conflicting set of *dictionaries*.

After discovering the *Truth*, my heart and mind were renewed and I saw how misguided and misled I'd been to put my hope and purpose in the world, even striving to be defined by it. The disheartening thing is, is that I grew up in a Christian home, understood Biblical principles, knew who God was, and had a relationship with Him but still fell victim to the wiles of the world. If this could happen to me, then it has surely happened to others. I am fortunate though to have been given a tough wake-up call. The right people came onto my path at the right time, and brought me back to where I was meant to be heading. Some even stirred greater things in me for the mission of the *Truth* that is in Jesus. This is mostly the purpose of this book, to ignite that stirring in someone else so they too may face up to that *renewing of the mind*, inevitably transforming their entire life. I hope for this book to be a catalyst of change for that someone who might also still be wondering in a hazy direction, having lost sight of the narrow path that leads to true life. May the message of this book, spark in you a flame that ignites your hunger for the *Truth*, that is in Jesus.

I have been crucified with Christ; it is no longer I who live, but Christ lives in me; and the life which I now live in the flesh I live by faith in the Son of God, who loved me and gave Himself for me. - Galatians 2:20

PURPOSE » IDENTITY » PURPOSE

God allowed me to suffer through, but also helped me to endure my decade of despair because He had a greater purpose for me. I needed to suffer in order to overcome. I strengthened in character and became more resilient to change, developing into *the strong woman* He needed me to be for the path thay lay ahead. Even though I had *wondered through the wilderness* during that decade of disaster, God never left me, He was always there. A greater purpose, His purpose for me, stood as a lighthouse of hope in the dark. He took me through the lowest and darkest moments of my entire life, caused me to beg and to cry out for mercy and healing, leaving me with no strength at all but His alone. I realised my need for God's *Truth* and my dependence on Him because that was the only thing that stood solid and made any sense.

Yea, though I walk through the valley of the shadow of death, I will fear no evil; For You *are* with me; Your rod and Your staff, they comfort me. Psalm 23:4

Through it all, a greater purpose emerged, finally providing me with the identity I had been searching for all that time. Once I realised that God had a unique plan and purpose for me and a place where I uniquely slotted in, with a unique message, I discovered even more purpose. I couldn't have been the person I am today, with the message I have to share, without enduring the trials that I did.

In hindsight, not during it all that's for sure, I am grateful for having suffered because I grew so much in character during that time. I realised so many things about myself, both my strengths and weaknesses, but most importantly received the affirmation that God was with me all the way through it. When I cried out to Him in my most rock bottom moments, He was there. To know that God was there beside me through it all and keeping me safe, is astounding. There were plenty of times because of reckless behaviour I should have been injured or even worse, but His angels protected me. Every vehicle I have ever owned, I have always asked God to send His angels to protect the driver and each passenger while on the road. To this day, not one person in my car has ever been hurt in the least. I owe this to the Lord. He has protected me and my passengers while journeying across many a land.

For He shall give His angels charge over you, To keep you in all your ways. - Psalm 91:11

ALL CREATION HAS PURPOSE » ALL CREATION TO GLORIFY GOD » ALL LIFE TO GLORIFY GOD

One of the most inspiring people of our generation is undeniably the *Life Without Limbs* author, Nick Vujicic. Nick was born without arms and legs to parents who were willing to face the many challenges that lay ahead. They lovingly accepted his condition right from the first bit of news regarding his medical condition because they understood life from God's perspective. Even though Nick refused to allow his physical condition to limit his active lifestyle, he did experience difficulties during childhood. Not only with the usual challenges of school and adolescence, but also with loneliness and depression. Nick naturally questioned why he had been born differently to other children, leading him to question the purpose of his life.

It so turns out that God had a great plan for Nick because Nick has since shared the gospel of God's love through Jesus Christ across the world to millions of people. God allowed Nick to be born with this condition, because without it he may never have reached so many people and impacted so many souls. Nick says, "If God can use a man without arms and legs to be His hands and feet, then He will certainly use any willing heart."

Just like Nick, each and every one of us has a purpose for which we were created. We might not understand it at first, or even recognise it, but if we earnestly seek God's will for our lives then it will be revealed to us.

For as we have many members in one body, but all the members do not have the same function, so we, *being* many, are one body in Christ, and individually members of one another. Having then gifts differing according to the grace that is given to us, *let us use them*. – Romans 12:4-6

Each one of us has a calling to fulfil what God has given us to do while on earth. This to me is the greatest honour, to serve Him through the gifts He has given us.

GOING FORWARD: THE *JOY* IN MY NEW IDENTITY

Now may the God of hope fill you with all joy and peace in believing, that you may abound in hope by the power of the Holy Spirit. - Romans 15:13

My declared identity as a child of God has confirmed my life's purpose. Finally, I know what I have to do, what my motivation is for getting up each day, what my future plans look like, and what I need to do with my time on earth. Can this be any more exciting? This is my JOY – my purpose - my mission - my life's work.

The moment I had personally grasped the gravity of why Jesus actually came to earth, as well as what it means for people who don't comprehend the gravity of His second coming, I was struck with an urgency to start sharing it.

Nothing is more important than the salvation of souls.

Nothing is more important than for people to know their Creator and how and why He loves them so much, but at the same time knowing what happens to those who deny their Creator.

Nothing is more important than to seek God, grow in understanding of who He is, and realise your need for a saviour. Without a saviour, you cannot even THINK about Heaven. If you cannot even THINK about eternity in Heaven, where does that leave your soul then for all eternity?

Jesus says in Revelations 21:6, "I will give of the fountain of the water of life freely to him who thirsts." Our only HOPE in eternal life lies in Jesus Christ.

THE GREAT COMMISSION » "COMMISSIONED"

Jesus said that "you shall receive power when the Holy Spirit has come upon you; and you shall be witnesses to Me in Jerusalem, and in all Judea and Samaria, and to the end of the earth. - Acts 1:8.

In 2019 I sensed a pressing connection to the word *commissioned*. Commissioned means *to produce specially to order (especially of a work of art); order or authorize (a person or organization) to do or produce something; bring (something newly produced) into working condition. The current English word is derived from the Latin word 'committere', which means 'entrust'.*

My path ahead is now clear. What JOY! I shall share the *Truth* with as many people as I can, using the gifts that God has given me. This is my commission – this is my mission.

You are the light of the world. A city that is set on a hill cannot be hidden. Nor do they light a lamp and put it under a basket, but on a lampstand, and it gives light to all *who are* in the house. Let your light so shine before men, that they may see your good works and glorify your Father in heaven. - Matthew 5: 14-16

THE MAGNITUDE OF THIS MISSION

With this mission comes an urgency. Even though it is joyful, it is pressing because not one person knows the day or hour, manner or place in which they will die. Our lives are so fragile and can be taken away in a second, with James 4:14 even describing our life as "vapour that appears for a little time and then vanishes away". This is how temporary our current existence on earth actually is.

If you die as an unrepented sinner, you die in sin. Therefore, you die in what separates you from God. Where does that leave you after you die? Still separated. And this is the part that is so urgent for me. The part of sharing with others how God sees sin, the magnitude of their repentance for these sins and how these sins were paid for. If you didn't pay for your sins, if you didn't take the punishment for these *crimes against God*, then who did? Any transgressional or illegal act on earth is first judged and then awarded a punishment, either a fine or a jail term. Why would this concept be any different to God, it isnt? After all, God is the one who gave humans legal framework in the first place, and is the One who implemented Law and Order so that we could see our illegal transgressions before our eyes. Without Law and Order, the human race would bury themselves in chaos.

While you are still alive on earth and while you are still breathing and able to confess with your own words, you must make the choice between life and death. This choice with your own words can lead to the difference between eternal life and eternal death. This is what drives me to write, to paint, to use my online accounts as a witnessing platform, to chat to people at the park, to start a local prayer group, to prayer walk in the streets, pray wherever I go, and constantly talk about God and speak *Truth* with whoever comes my way.

People need to know this. Your friends and family need to know this. My friends and family need to know this. The world needs to know this.

Sin cannot be in the presence of Holiness. Sin is filth in the eyes of God. We cannot stand before God in filthy, unwashed robes. Only through the blood of Jesus can any human be cleansed of this sin and their robes cleaned. Without it, you will "perish" (John 3:16).

> **So he said to me, "These are the ones who come out of the great tribulation, and washed their robes and made them white in the blood of the Lamb. – Revelation 7:14**

But you must profess faith in who Jesus is who He says He is. That He is the Son of the living God, the Saviour, the Messiah, the Truth, the Lamb, the King of kings, and Lord of lords. He is the only way to God, and the *Truth* to God. Jesus is the Truth to eternal life.

> **Death and life *are* in the power of the tongue. – Proverbs 18:21**

It is sad how many people I encounter who are oblivious to this. They live so comfortably with a thick veil over their eyes, not ever questioning what lies beyond the veil, making up every excuse under the sun not to come to terms with the questions that really matter. They allow human theories and opinions to give them an excuse for not searching any further than what they see in their local world or on their screens. *The Matrix* (1999) film perfectly illustrates this blind state of detachment that the world has from the *Truth*. For the character Neo (played by Keana Reeves) to see the truth of reality, the veil (in his case – 'the unplugging') that had been pulled over his eyes to blind him from the truth had to be removed. After searching earnestly, Neo was finally free from his blindness because of the choice he made to choose the truth rather than continue in blind comfort as he had before. Just as Neo had been set free from his life of denial, the *Truth* shall set us free.

> **Then Jesus said to those Jews who believed Him, "If you abide in My word, you are My disciples indeed. And you shall know the truth, and the truth shall make you free. – John 8: 31 – 32**

THE WEIGHT OF CHOICE

Revelations 20: 11-15 says, "Then I saw a great white throne and Him who sat on it, from whose face the earth and the heaven fled away. And there was found no place for them. And I saw the dead, small and great, standing before God, and books were opened. And another book was opened, which is *the Book* of Life. And the dead were judged according to their works, by the things which were written in the books. The sea gave up the dead who were in it, and Death and Hades delivered up the dead who were in them. And they were judged, each one according to his works. Then Death and Hades were cast into the lake of fire. This is the second death. And anyone not found written in the Book of Life was cast into the lake of fire."

I can't even begin to imagine this above scene.

Can you imagine this? *My tiny human brain cannot even comprehend it.*

Is this even humanly fathomable? An eternal lake of fire. As well as to be separated from our Father forever.

The curious thing is, is that no one has actually experienced life without the hand of God, so I don't think anyone could truly humanly imagine it. Creation is His garden and shows His labour, of which we live and breathe in, as well as the laws of a country that exist to keep us in order and peace. These are clear and obvious signs of God's work in our world. So, when some people say, "I am an atheist", they're indirectly saying, I am choosing to be blind to what is obvious to me.

I wonder how many of these *atheists* have really experienced a world with an absent God. None. Have any of them actually lived in a world without any law and order, where there is complete decay and chaos, no judiciary, no penalties, no law enforcement, or have any lived in a world without biological creativity. (There are many more areas, but law and creation are two easy obvious ones that demonstrates God's hand and so it is foolish to live in denial.), "The fool has said in his heart, *There is* no God." They are corrupt, They have done abominable works," (Psalm 14:1), "Because they hated knowledge And did not choose the fear of the Lord" (Proverbs 1:29).

The devil, who deceived them, was cast into the lake of fire and brimstone where the beast and the false prophet *are*. And they will be tormented day and night forever and ever. – Revelations 20:10

And He said to me, "It is done! I am the Alpha and the Omega, the Beginning and the End. I will give of the fountain of the water of life freely to him who thirsts. He who overcomes shall inherit all things, and I will be his God and he shall be My son. But the cowardly, unbelieving, abominable, murderers, sexually immoral, sorcerers, idolaters, and all liars shall have their part in the lake which burns with fire and brimstone, which is the second death. – Revelations 21: 6-8

The above passages terrify me – and put the fear of God into me. Matthew 10:28 confirms this so vividly, "And do not fear those who kill the body but cannot kill the soul. But rather fear Him who is able to destroy both soul and body in hell".

The fear of God is good and right because it keeps us "watchful and sober" (1 Thessalonians 5: 2-11). Proverbs 14:27 says that "the fear of the LORD *is* a fountain of life, To turn *one* away from the snares of death", and "In the fear of the LORD *there is* strong confidence, And His children will have a place of refuge" (Proverbs 14:26). The fear of the Lord is what encourages me to seek communion with Him daily, it is the *fear* that draws me back to Him continually when I feel I may have strayed, and it is fear that causes me to live a repentant heart.

For you yourselves know perfectly that the day of the Lord so comes as a thief in the night. For when they say, "Peace and safety!" then sudden destruction comes upon them, as labor pains upon a pregnant woman. And they shall not escape. But you, brethren, are not in darkness, so that this Day should overtake you as a thief. You are all sons of light and sons of the day. We are not of the night nor of darkness. Therefore let us not sleep, as others *do,* but let us watch and be sober. For those who sleep, sleep at night, and those who get drunk are drunk at night. But let us who are of the day be sober, putting on the breastplate of faith and love, and *as* a helmet the hope of salvation. For God did not appoint us to wrath, but to obtain salvation through our Lord Jesus Christ, who died for us, that whether we wake or sleep, we should live together with Him." Therefore comfort each other and edify one another, just as you also are doing. - 1 Thessalonians 5:2-11

When I read the book of Revelations, I am very quickly *sobered* as to the seriousness of what God is saying to humanity: sin is of the devil and only through the atoning blood of Jesus will you be saved from punishment. Just as the blood of a lamb (infant sheep) was used during the tenth plague in Egypt to *wash* the houses of God's people to save them from death, the same will happen to the people who have *washed* themselves with the blood of the Lamb, who is Jesus Christ.

When Jesus came into the region of Caesarea Philippi, He asked His disciples, saying, "Who do men say that I, the Son of Man, am?"

So they said, "Some *say* John the Baptist, some Elijah, and others Jeremiah or one of the prophets."

He said to them, "But who do you say that I am?"

Simon Peter answered and said, "You are the Christ, the Son of the living God."

Jesus answered and said to him, "Blessed are you, Simon Bar-Jonah, for flesh and blood has not revealed *this* to you, but My Father who is in heaven. And I also say to you that you are Peter, and on this rock I will build My church, and the gates of Hades shall not prevail against it. And I will give you the keys of the kingdom of heaven, and whatever you bind on earth will be bound in heaven, and whatever you loose on earth will be loosed in heaven. - Matthew 16: 13-19

THE MAGNITUDE OF GRACE

Because of the severity of choice and knowing the consequences of falling short as written about in the book of Revelations, there was a period where I struggled with the idea of *being righteous enough* to enter Heaven. I truly wrestled with this. I wrestled whether I was doing enough for God's Kingdom and if what I was doing was good enough. I struggled because I know how weak I am and that on my own I would never be righteous enough. I would never be Holy enough to stand before God. I am too weak, too flawed, too carnal.

It was then that I came across the reassurance that I needed, and the answer to my burden that I was carrying. As the impact of these words unravelled before my eyes, I started to weep. My burden of worry gradually subsided as I became overwhelmed at the power of this statement.

"My Grace is sufficient for you"

I said it over,

"My Grace is sufficient for you"

and over,

"My Grace is sufficient for you"

Again,

"May Grace is sufficient for you"

Wow!

And then Jesus says:

"My strength is made perfect in weakness".

And He said to me, "My grace is sufficient for you, for My strength is made perfect in weakness." – 2 Corinthians 12:9

My weakness is made perfect with His strength. *Thank you, Lord Jesus, thank you.* What a precious gift – His Grace. Without it I would fall short. He is all the righteousness I need, He is my righteousness. This is why I need Jesus. I need His gift of Grace. *Thank you, my Lord God.*

And now, may "The grace of the Lord Jesus Christ, and the love of God, and the communion of the Holy Spirit be with you all. Amen." - 2 Corinthians 13:14

A personal prayer for salvation

Lord Jesus, I believe you are the Christ. I believe you are the Son of the living God. I believe that you are my Lord and my Saviour. I believe that you died and shed your blood as atonement for my sins. I believe that you rose again. I confess my sins to You, repent of them and ask for forgiveness. Make me new and born again because only through You is eternal life. Show me Your Way to truly live for the Kingdom of God, here on Earth and in Heaven. Thank you for your gift of Grace. Amen.

CANDACE ANNE

Take my life and let it be

Lyrics: Frances R. Havergal, 1874

Music: Mozart

Take my life and let it be
Consecrated, Lord, to Thee.
*Take my moments and my days,
Let them flow in endless praise.

Take my hands and let them move
At the impulse of Thy love.
Take my feet and let them be
Swift and beautiful for Thee.

Take my voice and let me sing,
Always, only for my King.
Take my lips and let them be
Filled with messages from Thee.

Take my silver and my gold,
Not a mite would I withhold.
Take my intellect and use
Every pow'r as Thou shalt choose.

Take my will and make it Thine,
It shall be no longer mine.
Take my heart, it is Thine own,
It shall be Thy royal throne.

Take my love, my Lord, I pour
At Thy feet its treasure store.
Take myself and I will be
Ever, only, all for Thee.

My prayer going forward

For the true message of this book to be revealed to whoever reads it. The message being: *JESUS IS TRUTH,* and that only through Christ can we *truly* live both now and forever. He is the true light amidst all of this darkness. May this message fill your heart, your mind and your soul.

I also hope to inspire others to turn back to God if they have lost their way, or lost sight of the *Truth*, just like I did for a short while.

Brethren, if anyone among you wanders from the truth, and someone turns him back, let him know that he who turns a sinner from the error of his way will save a soul from death and cover a multitude of sins. – James 5:19-20

And now, *my ministry* begins.

But you be watchful in all things, endure afflictions, do the work of an evangelist, fulfil your ministry – 2 Timothy 4:5.

BIBLIOGRAPHY

Scripture taken from the New King James Version®. Copyright © 1982 by Thomas Nelson. Used by permission. All rights reserved.

Mere Christianity by CS Lewis © copyright CS Lewis Pte Ltd 1942, 1943, 1944, 1952. Used with permission.

Quote by Rick Warren, *The Purpose Driven Life* (2002). Used with permission by author.

LIST OF ILLUSTRATIONS

1. Charles Allan Gilbert, *All is Vanity*, (1892). Lithograph. (https://en.wikipedia.org/wiki/Charles_Allan_Gilbert)

2. *Temple Layout*, (2020). JPEG image. Based off the instructions in Exodus 25, Exodus 26 NKJV.

3. Candace Anne, *Jesus is Truth* illustration, (2020). Pen on paper.

Printed in the United States
by Baker & Taylor Publisher Services